WHEATLESS COOKING

WHEATLESS COOKING
(including gluten-free and sugar-free recipes)

Lynette Coffey

Ten Speed Press

1☉
Ten Speed Press
PO Box 7123
Berkeley, California 94707

First published in 1984 by Greenhouse Publications Pty Ltd,
Melbourne, Australia.

ISBN 0-89815-156-2

Photography by Paul Tremelling
Illustrations by Lowana Cummin
Typeset by Savage Type Pty Ltd, Brisbane

Printed in the United States of America

5 — 92

Contents

For Lee — your health is my reward many times over.

Foreword

In these modern times, science and our rapidly advancing technology have made life much more interesting and easier in lots of ways. This has also created problems for humanity. Mankind has seen more changes to the environment in the last fifty years than at any other time in the history of our planet.

Man in the past has been able to adapt to changes, genetically evolving over many hundreds and thousands of years. But in recent times — in the very short space of fifty years or so — our bodies have not had time to evolve and adapt. Therefore we have many diseases caused by our environmental changes and pollutants. Allergic reactions are a part of these disease states and affect us with many different symptoms, among them, hayfever, sinusitis, colds, diarrhoea, digestive disturbances, migraines, hyperactivity, depression, fatigue, skin conditions . . . the list could go on and on. The allergic substances include heavy metals such as mercury, copper, lead and zinc, as well as those chemicals that have found their way into our food and water, for example pesticides, artificial colourings, preservatives, petrochemicals and artificial flavourings.

We can go some way to avoiding these, by seeking out foods grown free of pesticides and by careful reading of labels, but to really aid our immune and digestive systems this is not always enough. Deficiencies of trace elements and vitamins may also play a part and by taking supplements of these we can help our bodies in eliminating toxins, and as a result we can improve the function of our detoxifying organs and thereby regain and maintain our wellbeing.

Some of us, however are even allergic to different types of food and this can produce severe disease symptoms. Lynette Coffey is a dedicated mother who suffered, along with her son, the problems caused by his allergies, particularly to wheat. She then experienced the relief of seeing those symptoms disappear within only a few days when the causes of the allergic conditions were pinpointed and avoided.

Her book will be of great benefit and encouragement to those who experience the same difficulties and frustrations. She has shown that it is possible to have food that is just as enjoyable, even without something as basic as wheat, and her book will give heart to those faced with the real difficulties of both finding and preparing food free from wheat.

Dr Malcolm D. Hutchinson, D.O.N.D.
Osteopath and Natural Therapist

Where it all began

At the age of three my eldest son, Lee, was allergic to dairy produce (cow's milk, butter, cheese and yoghurt) and eggs. He had suffered from unexplained constant diarrhoea since birth. He had also had numerous ear and throat infections, which became more and more difficult to clear up. At one stage Lee was on to his third dose of antibiotics and medicine to dry up the mucus, in a little over a month. Our family doctor was so concerned that he suggested we take Lee to a specialist.

We went to the specialist three weeks later. He recommended that Lee have his tonsils and adenoids removed, and drainage tubes placed in his ears. The specialist also prescribed another course of antibiotics and drying-up medicine because Lee had another ear and throat infection. The operation was to be performed as soon as the infection had cleared. My husband, Roland, and I were greatly concerned about Lee having the operation, not only because he was so young, but also because he was an asthmatic.

In desperation we took Lee to see a Naturopath, Malcolm Hutchinson. He diagnosed Lee as being allergic to dairy produce, eggs (yes, we knew that), kapok, rye and wheat! We were sceptical, but we were also desperate. For the next six weeks Lee's diet was restricted to meat, vegetables and fruit. It was a very frustrating time for us all. Lee craved after wheat products to the extent of licking breadcrumbs from the table, and trying to steal bread and biscuits from the cupboard. I searched for some alternative that I could give Lee. All I found were rice cakes, which he refused to eat. As the days passed, and I spent hour upon hour in the supermarket reading labels, I came to realise just how much our daily food depends on wheat flour.

1

Lee's desire for bread, especially, was becoming extreme. Finally a health food store suggested we try a Gluten Free Bread Mix. I made the bread the same day and he loved it. By this time I could see the improvement in Lee's health, but after eating the bread he took a step backwards. I eventually found out that Lee is not allergic to gluten, he is allergic to wheat and wheat gluten. (Gluten Free bread is processed from wheat flour with the gluten removed.)

Wheat allergy is becoming more common in recent times. It is not just a 'fad diagnosis', it's a very real problem. In my opinion, wheat allergies are being created by our unnecessary over-use, and by the introduction of wheat into babies' diets too early. Wheat certainly is a splendid grain, but there are many other grains with so much to offer that we really should not ignore them. The healthiest diet is one which includes a wide variety of nutritious foods. We have known this for years but have neglected to extend this rule to the grains we eat. It's only recently that we have started to realise the benefit of eating multi-grain bread, let alone the new tastes and textures that these grains have to offer.

Six weeks after his wheat allergy was diagnosed, I took Lee back to the doctor who said he had never seen Lee's ears so clear — ever. He doubted that he would need the operation if they stayed that way. As Lee's health improved his allergies, with the exception of wheat, started to disappear. I slowly introduced 100 per cent rye bread (see cooking notes page 6) into his diet and he tolerated it very well. At last Lee's fondest wish had come true ... a piece of toast with honey.

Lee's younger brother Glen's birthday was coming and I wanted to bake a cake that Lee could eat as well. I couldn't find a recipe for a wheatless cake anywhere, so I started experimenting. Lots of attempts were thrown out. The last one before Glen's birthday held together, so I iced it, stuck a candle in it, and threw it away afterwards as well. It tasted terrible! I couldn't help but wonder how many people were having the same problems. Had I been the one with the allergy, I would have given up there and then, but I wanted Lee to be able to enjoy the same type of food that all his family and friends were eating. I was sure there must be others who felt the same.

I decided if I could produce food that looked and tasted as good as food made from wheat flour, I would put the recipes in a book and share them with others.

Lots of disasters later, I had finally learnt the characteristics of the flours I was using, and subsequently, where their best application would be. I then had to work out the ratio of ingredients to each other. The amount of milk and butter, for instance, varies according to which type of flour is being used.

At about this time a friend, Shirley Fisher, offered her assistance, which I gratefully accepted. Shirley is a Home Economics teacher and her help and advice proved invaluable.

What we have finally ended up with are wheatless alternatives to a wide range of products including cakes, biscuits, bread, pizzas, pies and pancakes, etc. These products look and taste as good as food produced with wheat. In lots of cases they actually taste better, while at the same time being nutritionally superior to white flour products. All alternate flours (with the exception of cornflour and potato flour) are wholegrain flours, yet by selecting and combining flours carefully, we have been able to achieve a 'white-flour effect', where desirable (for example in quite a lot of the cakes).

I hope you will enjoy using this book. If you have a wheat allergy or even a gluten allergy, I feel certain you will get satisfaction from being able to share your 'goodies' with family and friends, but most of all, you will be able to enjoy all those things that you have probably been going without.

Lynette Coffey

At the time of this book going to the publisher, Lee has just turned 5. Since he has been off wheat, *all* of his other allergies have disappeared. He has not had any tonsilitis or ear infections in the past two years, and subsequently has not needed any antibiotics in that time either. He has had one bout of diarrhoea when I tried re-introducing wheat products late last year. He has also had five mild asthma attacks. Each of these were within 24 hours of eating wheat products. If Lee has a small amount of wheat, it is followed by a mild asthma attack. If he has a larger amount, his body rejects it entirely as he has diarrhoea lasting about a week. I am a sceptic no longer. People *can* be allergic to what we refer to as the 'staff of life' — and I believe there are many more of us than anybody realises, with symptoms ranging from the extreme, like Lee, to just never feeling 'quite right'.

Gluten Allergy vs Wheat Allergy

This book has been specially prepared for those with a wheat allergy. However, many people who may find it useful have a gluten allergy (they are called Coeliacs).

Grains containing gluten are wheat, rye, oats, barley, although wheat gluten allergy is by far the most common gluten allergy.

All the recipes in this book are free of wheat gluten. Many recipes are free of all types of gluten and are marked accordingly, both in the index and on the recipe.

Flours free of gluten are rice, soy flour, pure maize corn flour, corn meal, millet meal and potato flour.

Buckwheat flour contains a gluten analogue which a lot of people with gluten allergies can tolerate. Recipes containing buckwheat flour are also marked in the index. Do not be confused by the name buckwheat; it is not a wheat and can be tolerated by those with a wheat allergy, unless they are also allergic to buckwheat.

Gluten-free Flour

It is important to remember that this flour is made from *wheat*, which has had all the gluten removed. It is suitable for those who have a gluten allergy but can tolerate wheat, but is *unsuitable* for those with a wheat allergy. It is *not* used in recipes in this book.

Foods that may contain wheat flour, and some alternatives

- soft icing (pure icing sugar has no flour)
- gravy powder
- stuffing
- chicken noodle soup
- all packaged and tinned soups
- pastes (fish paste, ham paste, etc.)
- pasta (remember that semolina too is processed from wheat) — use a 100 per cent buckwheat spaghetti or rice instead
- bread
- rye bread (most rye breads have a large proportion of wheat flour added — read the list of ingredients carefully)
- cakes and cake mixes
- biscuits — except rice crackers
- crispbreads — except 100% rye flour crispbreads (Finn Crisp, Rykrisp, Ry, etc.), and rice crackers (eg Hol-Grain Brown Rice Thins)
- muesli
- instant puddings
- custard powder
- breakfast cereals except 'Kellogg's Corn Flakes', 'Kellogg's Rice Krispies'
- batter (chicken rolls, Chinese appetisers, grilled and fried fish, potato cakes)
- sausages
- some cold meats (salami, strasburg, etc.)
- most corn flour (buy only pure maize corn flour)
- breadcrumbs
- chocolate (but read the label)

Read all labels carefully when buying. All products should list their ingredients. Any of the following may indicate the presence of wheat or wheat flour: flour, starch, thickening, corn flour, bran, wheat germ.

Other allergies

Some readers may be allergic to ingredients other than the cereals and flours used in the recipes in this book, especially to dairy produce. They will need to replace these ingredients.

Milk: Most recipes will work using any form of milk. If you have a dairy produce allergy you will need to use one of the various soya bean substitutes available (soymilk, fresh of powdered), or goat's milk. (Goat's milk, yoghurt and cheese are usually available at health food stores.)

Butter: If you cannot tolerate butter, or would prefer not to use it, substitute whatever margarine, etc., you would normally use. Most margarines contain a certain amount of cow's milk, so if you are allergic to dairy produce, make sure that you buy a margarine that is free of cow's milk.

Notes on Grains and Flours

Keeping flour: To gain maximum nutritional value from your flours, try to buy the freshest flour possible and keep it in the freezer until needed. Flour does not freeze solid and can be used straight from the freezer.

Rye flour: You will hear of white and dark rye flours. The white rye flour has either had the bran removed or white wheat flour added to it. The rye flour referred to here is the wholegrain, stone ground, dark variety.

Oatmeal: This is produced by grinding the oat groat to a meal-like consistency.

Soy flour: The best soy flour is heat treated, full fat (debittered). It is produced from the best quality soya beans that have been cleaned, dehulled and cracked before milling. It is rich in protein and gluten free.

Brown rice flour: This is a wholegrain rice flour. There is very little difference in the finished product whether brown rice flour or white rice flour is used, but I use brown rice flour exclusively as it is nutritionally better.

Corn flour: All corn flour *must be* pure maize corn flour. It is milled from the whole maize. All other corn flours are processed from wheat.

Barley flour: I use the 100 per cent wholegrain, stone ground barley flour.

Buckwheat flour: This stone ground product belongs to the rhubarb and dock family and so is not a cereal at all.

Hulled millet: This is white French millet with the husk removed.

Maize meal: Maize meal, corn meal, yellow corn meal and polenta are all different names for the same ingredient. They are produced from the outer region of the maize seed.

Millet meal: I use the stone ground product. This grain is a great source of vitamin B17 and has similar protein to wheat. It is often referred to as the King of Grains.

Potato flour: This is simply dried potato and has the consistency of corn flour.

Rolled oats: These are produced by rolling the whole grain into a flake-like product.

Rye flakes/barley flakes: These, too, are rolled and are interchangeable with rolled oats. If you are allergic to one of them, just substitute one of the others for the offending ingredient.

Special notes

a *Semolina* is processed from wheat. Pasta made from semolina should be avoided.

b *Gluten free flour* is marketed in health food shops, chemists and supermarkets. Remember that this product is produced from *wheat* but has had all the gluten removed.

Other useful cereals

Linseed grain — is a delicious addition to bread and biscuits and may be ground into meal.

Alfalfa grain — is suitable for sprouting.

Sesame seed — is high in nutrients. It has a pleasant taste and aroma and is ideal as toppings for bread or similar.

Soya beans — are high in protein but may be indigestible to some. This can be overcome to some extent by sprouting prior to cooking and not combining them with carbohydrate products.

Soybean flakes — may be used to replace rolled oats, etc., in muesli, cakes, biscuits and breads as a gluten free alternative, and may be added to stews and casseroles.

Rice flakes — are delicious as a rice pudding.

Natural lecithin — is from the heart of the soya bean. It is best in its concentrated granular form, which is 95 per cent pure lecithin, as opposed to the lecithin meal or lecithin granules which may have only 19 to 20 per cent lecithin and may even be loaded with sugar. This lecithin may be used as a dietary supplement, added to cereals, or to drinks like egg nogs and milk shakes, or added to soups, hamburgers, casseroles.

Soy grits — are prepared from soya beans by being granulated, steamed, partially defatted and dried. They are a very palatable, nutrient-rich food. They may be eaten dry as an alternative to granulated nuts, or used as a component in muesli or vegetable casseroles.

Rye grain, organically grown — is used in grinding your own flour, or sprouting. It may be boiled to produce a breakfast treat, or as an addition to salads. It should be used like rice.

Kibbled rye — is produced by cracking the whole rye grain. It may be called kibbled or cracked rye.

Buckwheat kernels — have had only the black outer husk removed. They can be cooked as a porridge, boiled and used as a side dish with meat, or used in dumplings.

Sunflower kernels — are a delightful seed which can be used in biscuits, cakes and salads, or for a nibble.

The product information given above was supplied by Lowan Whole Foods who distribute throughout health food stores. These products are also available in selected supermarkets under the name of The Old Grain Mill.

Comparative Food Value of Cereals
(per 100 grams)

	Protein	Fat	Carbohydrate	Energy	Energy	Calcium	Iron
	g	g	g	Cal	kj	mg	mg
Barley	12.0	1.5	71	342	1,431	40	5
Maize	10.0	4.5	70	360	1,506	20	4
Millet — pearl	11.0	3.0	70	351	1,468	20	5
Millet — finger	8.0	1.3	72	332	1,389	350	5
Sorghum	10.0	3.0	70	347	1,452	25	5
Oats	12.0	9.0	69	405	1,694	55	4
Brown rice	6.0	2.0	81	366	1,531	40	2
White rice	6.0	0.5	80	348	1,456	24	1
Rye	10.0	2.5	70	342	1,431	55	4
Whole wheat	12.0	2.0	70	326	1,364	60	6

Based on a table published in *You And Your Food*, F. W. Clements & J. F. Rogers

Notes on Sugar-free Cooking

Wheat-free, sugar-free cakes and biscuits have neither the binding quality of wheat gluten, nor the 'stickiness' of sugar. They should therefore be handled with a little bit of care. Always line the bottom of cake tins with paper. Loosen cakes or biscuits in their tins and trays while still warm, but leave them to cool before removing them.

When buying ingredients for the sugar-free recipes, make sure the goods you are buying do not have any added sugar. This is especially important when buying dried fruit. All juices and canned fruit should be unsweetened.

If you would like to serve sugar-free food, but the rest of the family and friends are not ready for them, try adding some sugar to the recipes. Then, each time you make it again, decrease the amount of sugar slightly. The results can be more rewarding than trying to drastically change your diet overnight.

Notes on Egg-free Cooking

There are several possible egg substitutes, such as:
- 3 tablespoons puréed apple for each egg;
- 1 medium banana for each egg;
- omitting yolk, using white and 2 tablespoons milk;
- omitting yolk, using double quantity of egg whites.

The suitability of the above individual egg substitutes will vary according to the recipe you are using, but do try them.

Cooking notes

Cooking times

All cooking times and temperatures given in this book are for use with gas ovens. If you are using electric you may need to increase the temperature slightly.

Comparative oven temperature guide

Description	Gas		Electric	
	°C	°F	°C	°F
Cool	100	200	110	225
Very slow	120	250	120	250
Slow	150	300	150	300
Moderately slow	160	325	170	340
Moderate	175	350	200	400
Moderately hot	190	375	220	425
Hot	200	400	230	450
Very hot	230	450	250	475

Comparative liquid measures

Metric	Imperial
5 ml	1 teaspoon
20 ml	1 tablespoon
60 ml	2 fluid ounces (¼ cup)
125 ml	4 fluid ounces (½ cup)
250 ml	8 fluid ounces (1 cup)
625 ml	1 pint (20 fluid ounces)

Comparative solid measures

Avoirdupois	Metric
1 ounce	30 g
4 ounces	125 g
8 ounces	250 g
12 ounces	375 g
16 ounces	500 g
24 ounces	750 g
32 ounces	1000 g (1 kg)

Abbreviations used in this book

g   = gram/s
kg   = kilogram/s
cm   = centimetres
mm   = millimetres
"   = inches

Baking powder

I make my own baking powder. It is more economical and is free of any unnecessary additives. The recipe is as follows:
2 parts cream of tartar
1 part bicarbonate of soda
Mix thoroughly and store in an airtight container.

Cakes

Apple and walnut cake

2 cups raw apple cut into small cubes
2 eggs
½ cup raw sugar
⅓ cup oil
½ cup chopped walnuts

1 teaspoon vanilla
½ cups rice flour
½ teaspoon cinnamon
pinch salt
¼ teaspoon baking soda

1 Preheat oven to 175°C (350°F).
2 Grease 20 cm (8") cake tin.
3 Lightly beat eggs.
4 Combine apple, eggs, sugar, oil, walnuts and vanilla.
5 Sift flour, cinnamon, salt and baking soda.
6 Add flour mixture to apple mixture.
7 Mix well.
8 Pour into prepared tin.
9 Bake for approximately 60 minutes.

Boiled fruit cake

375 g/12 ounces mixed dried fruit, eg
    sultanas, currants, raisins, glacé
    cherries
60 g/2 ounces chopped dates
125 g/4 ounces butter
1 cup raw sugar
1 tablespoon golden syrup
1 cup water

1 egg
1 cup rye flour
1 cup rice flour
2 tablespoons soy flour
2 teaspoons baking powder
pinch salt
⅓ cup chopped walnuts

1 Line a 20 cm (8") round cake tin with two thicknesses of grease-proof paper.
2 Place mixed fruit, dates, butter, sugar, golden syrup and water in saucepan.
3 Stir over low heat until butter melts, bring to the boil and boil for 2 minutes.
4 Allow to become completely cold.
5 Preheat oven to 160°C (325°F).
6 Add lightly beaten egg to boiled fruit mixture.
7 Add sifted dry ingredients and walnuts, mix well.
8 Place in prepared tin and bake for 2 hours, or until cooked when tested.

Carob cake

125 g/4 ounces butter
¾ cup castor sugar
⅔ cup steamed mashed potato (cool)
⅓ cup carob powder
2 eggs (lightly beaten)

1 cup rice flour
½ cup soy flour
2 teaspoons baking powder
⅓ cup milk

1 Preheat oven to 175°C (350°F).
2 Grease 20 cm (8") cake tin.
3 Cream butter and sugar in large bowl.
4 Add mashed potato, beat well.
5 Gradually beat in eggs.
6 Sift flours, baking powder and carob together.
7 Fold in flour mixture alternately with milk, blend well.
8 Pour into prepared tin and bake for 40–50 minutes.

Carrot walnut cake

1½ cups brown rice flour
½ cup soy flour
3 teaspoons baking powder
1 teaspoon bicarbonate of soda
½–1 cup castor sugar
¾ cup steamed mashed carrot
⅓ cup raw grated carrot

½ cup crushed pineapple
* (undrained)*
2 eggs
⅓ cup oil
1 teaspoon vanilla
½ cup chopped walnuts

1 Preheat oven to 175°C (350°F).
2 Grease 20 cm x 10 cm (8" x 4") loaf tin and line the bottom with greaseproof paper.
3 Sift flours, baking powder, bicarbonate of soda, sugar into a large bowl.
4 Add pineapple, carrot, eggs, oil and vanilla.
5 Beat until combined.
6 Stir in the nuts.
7 Pour into prepared loaf tin and bake for 60–70 minutes.

Variation
For a sugar free alternative omit sugar, use unsweetened pineapple.

Chocolate cake

¾ cup soy flour
¾ cup brown rice flour
2 teaspoons baking powder
2 tablespoons cocoa
1 teaspoon vanilla

2 eggs
125 g/4 ounces butter (melted)
½ cup milk
⅔ cup castor sugar

1 Preheat oven to 175°C (350°F).
2 Grease 20 cm (8") cake tin.
3 Sift flours and baking powder.
4 Combine all ingredients and beat for 3 minutes with an electric mixer.
5 Pour into prepared tin and bake for approximately 50 minutes.

Coconut cake

1 cup barley flour
½ cup soy flour
2 teaspoons baking powder
1 cup sugar
1 cup coconut

125 g/4 ounces melted butter
½ cup milk
2 eggs
1 teaspoon vanilla

1 Grease a 20 cm (8") cake tin.
2 Preheat oven to 175°C (350°F).
3 Place all ingredients in a large bowl, and beat for 3 minutes with an electric mixer.
4 Pour into greased cake tin and bake for approximately 80 minutes.

Opposite: flours, grains and cereals used in the recipes. From top to bottom and left to right: millet meal, brown rice flour, buckwheat flour, millet grain, brown rice, buckwheat grain, soy flour, maize meal, barley grain, rye grain, oats groats, barley flakes, rye flakes, rolled oats, barley flour, rye flour and oatmeal.

Overleaf: biscuits and slices. In a clockwise direction from the top of the page: rye shortbread, fruit and nut slice, no-bake cookies, nut oat slice and oat crisps, barley shortbread (light colour) and rye shortbread (dark colour).

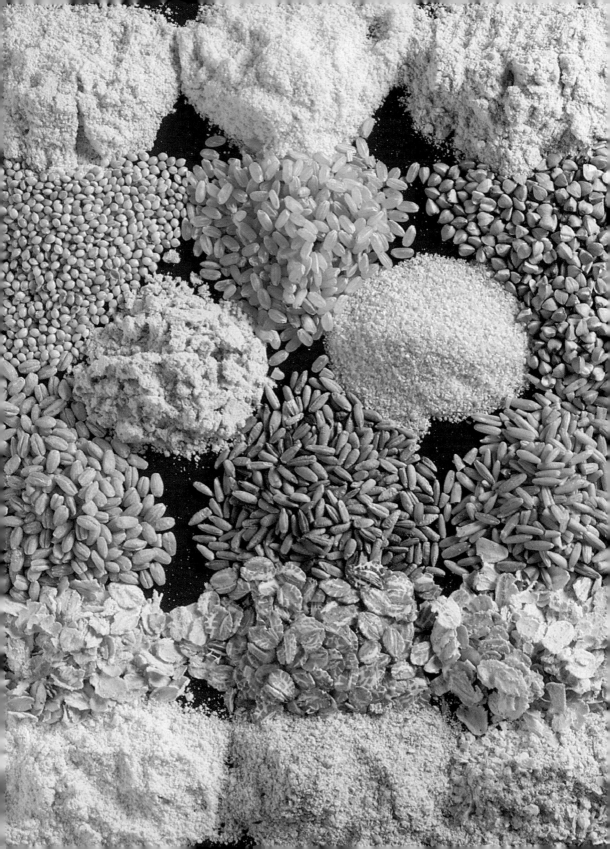

German apple cake

Gluten Free

60 g/2 ounces butter
1/3 cup sugar
1 egg
1/2 teaspoon vanilla
2/3 cup rice flour
1/3 cup soy flour

2 teaspoons baking powder
1/4 cup milk
3 medium apples
juice of 1 lemon
cinnamon and extra sugar

1 Preheat oven to 175°C (350°F).
2 Grease 20 cm (8") round cake tin.
3 Cream butter and sugar in large bowl.
4 Add egg and vanilla and beat well.
5 Sift flours and baking powder.
6 Add half flour mixture to egg mixture and beat.
7 Add milk and remaining flour alternately.
8 Spread over base of tin.
9 Peel, quarter and remove core from apples.
10 Cut into thin slices and squeeze lemon juice over.
11 Arrange slices over cake mixture (see diagram below).
12 Bake for approximately 60 minutes.
13 Sprinkle with extra sugar and cinnamon while still hot.

This cake looks spectacular and tastes great — without being too sweet.

Variation
For a sugar free alternative omit sugar from recipe, blend 1 apple in a food processor, add apple with 2 eggs and vanilla, reduce milk to 1 tablespoon and sprinkle with cinnamon only.

Opposite: from left to right, German apple cake and hazelnut torte.

Overleaf: beginning at the top of the page, in a clockwise direction: chocolate cake, sultana cake, strawberry yoghurt slice and glacé fruit cake.

Glacé fruit & nut cake

2 tablespoons rye flour
3 tablespoons pure maize corn flour
pinch baking powder
500 g/16 ounces honey glacé fruit
  salad (available at health food
  stores)
250 g/8 ounces dates

125 g/4 ounces whole blanched
  almonds
125 g/4 ounces shelled brazil nuts
90 g/3 ounces butter
⅓ cup raw sugar
2 eggs

1　Preheat oven to 150°C (300°F).
2　Grease and line with greaseproof paper a 20 cm x 10 cm (8" x 4") loaf tin.
3　Remove seeds and chop dates.
4　Chop glacé fruits.
5　Combine fruits and nuts.
6　Beat softened butter, sugar, eggs, flours, baking powder until smooth.
7　Add to fruit and nut mixture. Mix well.
8　Press into loaf tin.
9　Cover with foil, leaving room for expansion.
10　Bake for approximately 2 hours.
11　Leave cake covered until cold.
12　Remove from tin.
13　Leave for 3 days before cutting.
14　Cut with a sharp, serrated knife.

Gluten Free

Hazelnut torte

3 eggs, separated
1 cup castor sugar
250 g/8 ounces softened butter
1½ cups potato flour

2½ teaspoons baking powder
125 g/4 ounces ground hazelnuts
  (available at health food stores)
juice and rind of ½ lemon

1　Preheat oven to 160°C (325°F).
2　Grease and dust with potato flour a 20 cm (8") cake tin.
3　Beat egg whites until fluffy.
4　Gradually add sugar while continuing to beat, then put aside.
5　Lightly beat softened butter and egg yolks.
6　Add potato flour and baking powder, beat for 3 minutes on high speed.
7　Add egg white mixture, ground hazelnuts, lemon juice and rind to flour mixture.
8　Mix well.
9　Pour into prepared tin.
10　Bake for approximately 70 minutes.

Hearty boiled fruit cake

2 cups mixed dried fruit, eg sultanas,
    currants, dates and glacé cherries
1/3 cup pitted dates (chopped)
125 g/4 ounces butter
1 1/4 cups orange juice (apple juice or
    water)
2 eggs (lightly beaten)

3/4 cup soy flour
1 1/2 cups brown rice flour
3 teaspoons baking powder
1/3 cup almonds (slivered or coarsely
    chopped)

1 Place mixed fruit, dates, butter and juice or water in saucepan.
2 Stir over low heat until butter melts, bring to the boil and boil for
   2 minutes.
3 Allow to become completely cold.
4 Preheat oven to 160°C (325°F).
5 Line a 20 cm (8") cake tin with two thicknesses of greaseproof paper.
6 Add lightly beaten eggs to boiled fruit mixture.
7 Add sifted dry ingredients and almonds, mix well.
8 Place in prepared tin and bake for 1 1/4 hours, or until cooked when
   tested.

Jubilee cake

2 cups mixed dried fruit (see above)
1 cup rice flour
1 cup barley flour or oatmeal
3 teaspoons baking powder
2 rounded tablespoons butter

1 tablespoon sugar
grated rind of 1 small lemon
2 eggs
just over 3/4 cup milk

1 Soak mixed fruit overnight in a cup of water and drain before use.
2 Preheat oven to 175°C (350°F).
3 Grease a 20 cm x 10 cm (8" x 4") loaf tin.
4 Sift flours and baking powder.
5 Rub butter into flours.
6 Add rest of dry ingredients.
7 Lightly beat eggs and milk, add to dry ingredients.
8 Bake for approximately 50–60 minutes, or until cooked when tested
   with a skewer.
9 When cool cut into thick slices and spread with butter.

Variation
For a sugar free alternative omit sugar.

Plain cake

1¼ cups rice flour   *125 g/4 ounces melted butter*
½ cup soy flour   *⅔ cup milk*
2½ teaspoons baking powder   *2 eggs*
½ cup castor sugar   *1 teaspoon vanilla*

1 Preheat oven to 175°C (350°F).
2 Grease a 20 cm (8") cake tin.
3 Sift flours and baking powder.
4 Combine all ingredients in a large bowl and beat for 3 minutes, with an electric mixer.
5 Pour into prepared cake tin.
6 Bake for 50–60 minutes.

Variation
For a lemon or orange cake, add juice and rind of either one lemon or one orange. Add milk to the juice to make up the ⅔ cup of milk required for the recipe.

Pumpkin cake

½ cup softened butter   *2 teaspoons cinnamon*
½ cup raw sugar   *½ teaspoon bicarbonate of soda*
2 eggs   *pinch salt*
1 cup grated peeled pumpkin   *½ cup chopped pumpkin seeds*
1 tablespoon honey   *1¼ cups millet flour (millet meal)*

1 Preheat oven to 160°C (325°F).
2 Grease a 20 cm (8") cake tin, or small loaf tin.
3 Cream sugar and butter in large bowl, add eggs and mix.
4 Add all other ingredients and mix well.
5 Pour into cake tin and bake for approximately 50 minutes.
6 When cold, cake could be iced and decorated with chopped pumpkin seeds.

Spicy pumpkin cake

Gluten Free
Sugar Free

¾ cup sultanas
¾ cup raisins
½ cup mixed dried peel
¾ cup finely chopped dried apricots
1 cup unsweetened orange or apple juice
¾ cup steamed mashed pumpkin (cold)

2 eggs (lightly beaten)
1¼ cups brown rice flour
½ cup soy flour
3 teaspoons baking powder
1 teaspoon mixed spice

1 Combine fruit and juice in saucepan, bring to the boil and simmer for 1 minute and cool.
2 Preheat oven to 165°C (325°F).
3 Lightly grease a 20 cm (8") round cake tin and line the bottom with greaseproof paper.
4 Combine pumpkin, eggs and fruit mixture and beat until smooth.
5 Sift flours, baking powder and spice together.
6 Stir flour mixture into fruit mixture and beat well.
7 Bake for approximately 1 hour or until cooked when tested.

Sponge

Gluten Free

4 eggs
pinch salt
½ cup castor sugar
1 teaspoon vanilla

½ cup pure maize corn flour
¼ cup soy flour
1 teaspoon baking powder

1 Grease two 18 cm (7") sponge tins.
2 Preheat oven to 200°C (400°F).
3 Separate eggs.
4 Beat egg whites and salt lightly.
5 Gradually beat in castor sugar, continue beating until glossy.
6 Beat in yolks and vanilla.
7 Sift flours and baking powder twice.
8 Fold into egg mixture.
9 Pour into prepared sponge tins.
10 Bake for approximately 30 minutes.

Variation

This mixture can be used to make cup cakes by half filling cases, and reducing the cooking time to 15–20 minutes. When cool decorate with icing and top with chopped nuts, a glazed cherry on each.

Sultana apple cake

1⅓ cups stewed apple (drained)
¾ cup sultanas (soaked in water for
   2 hours or overnight then drained
   and finely chopped)
⅓ cup oil
2 eggs
1 teaspoon vanilla

1½ cups brown rice flour
½ cup soy flour
3 teaspoons baking powder
1 teaspoon cinnamon
1 cup raw apple cut into small cubes
½ cup chopped nuts (optional)

1 Preheat oven to 175°C (350°F).
2 Grease 20 cm (8") cake tin.
3 Combine stewed apple, sultanas, oil, eggs and vanilla and beat well.
4 Sift flours, cinnamon and baking powder.
5 Add flour mixture to apple mixture and mix well.
6 Fold in raw apple and nuts.
7 Pour into prepared tin.
8 Bake for approximately 60 minutes.

Serving suggestions
Slice cake in half and fill with apple and rhubarb, or apple purée. Serve with cream or yoghurt.

Sultana cake

1¼ cups rice flour
½ cup soy flour
2½ teaspoons baking powder
½ cup castor sugar
125 g/4 ounces melted butter
⅔ cup milk

2 eggs
1 teaspoon vanilla
1 cup sultanas
peel of one orange (grated)
almonds to decorate

1 Preheat oven to 175°C (350°F).
2 Grease a 20 cm (8") cake tin.
3 Sift flours and baking powder.
4 Combine all ingredients except sultanas, orange peel and almonds in a large bowl.
5 Beat for 3 minutes with an electric mixer.
6 Add remaining ingredients except almonds and mix well.
7 Pour into prepared tin, decorate with almonds.
8 Bake for 50–60 minutes.

Variation
For a sugar free alternative increase sultanas to 1¼ cups, soak sultanas overnight in 1 cup of water, blend drained sultanas and 1 ripe banana in a food processor, omit sugar and reduce milk to ½ cup.

Loaves and Muffins

Banana nut loaf

125 g/4 ounces butter
½ cup sugar
2 eggs (beaten)
1 cup mashed banana
1 teaspoon lemon juice
½ cup chopped walnuts

½ cup rice flour
½ cup soy flour
1 cup oatmeal
3 teaspoons baking powder
½ teaspoon bicarbonate of soda

1 Preheat oven to 175°C (350°F).
2 Grease a 20 cm x 10 cm (8" x 4") loaf tin.
3 Cream butter and sugar in large bowl.
4 Add egg gradually and beat well.
5 Add lemon juice to mashed banana and beat into butter mixture.
6 Fold in walnuts.
7 Sift flours, baking powder and bicarbonate of soda and fold into mixture.
8 Tip into prepared tin and bake for approximately 1 hour.

Variation
For a sugar free alternative increase banana to 1¼ cups and omit sugar.

Gluten Free

Date and nut loaf
makes 2 loaves

1 cup chopped dates
½ cup chopped walnuts
½ cup sultanas
1 cup raw sugar
1 teaspoon bicarbonate of soda

1 tablespoon butter
1 cup boiling water
2 cups rice flour (sifted)
½ teaspoon salt
1 egg (lightly beaten)

1 Preheat oven to 175°C (350°F).
2 Grease two nut loaf tins (or use cleaned soup cans)
3 Place dates, walnuts, sultanas, sugar, bicarbonate of soda and butter in a large bowl.
4 Pour boiling water into bowl and mix well.
5 Add rice flour, salt and egg and mix well.
6 Pour into prepared tins.
7 Stand upright on first rung in oven.
8 Bake for 60–70 minutes, or until cooked when tested with a skewer.
9 When cool, slice and spread with butter.

Date muffins

(use as a scone)
makes 12

2 cups soy flour
1 tablespoon baking powder
1 cup chopped dates

1 cup milk
2 eggs

1 Preheat oven to 175°C (350°F).
2 Grease muffin tray.
3 Sift flour and baking powder.
4 Add remaining ingredients and mix well.
5 Pour into muffin tray and bake for approximately 20–30 minutes.
6 Serve buttered or with jam and cream.

Millet-apricot loaf

1⅓ cups milk
1 cup rye flakes
½ cup sultanas
½–¾ cup raw sugar (depending on
   taste)

½ cup chopped dried apricots
¾ cup millet flour
¾ cup rice flour (sifted)
¼ cup sesame seeds (optional)
3 teaspoons baking powder

1 Mix milk, rye flakes, sultanas, sugar and apricots and soak for 3
   hours or preferably overnight.
2 Add millet flour, rice flour, sesame seeds and baking powder.
3 Mix well.
4 Preheat oven to 175°C (350°F).
5 Grease a 20 cm x 10 cm (8" x 4") loaf tin and line with greaseproof
   paper.
6 Pour mixture in and bake for approximately 50–60 minutes.
7 When cool this loaf can be sliced and buttered or eaten plain.

This is quite a heavy loaf — packed with nutrition

Prune tea loaf

1 tablespoon butter
1 tablespoon golden syrup (or Karo Syrup)
1⅓ cups oatmeal
½ cup cornmeal
½ teaspoon bicarbonate of soda

1 teaspoon baking powder
½ cup chopped prunes
1 tablespoon brown sugar
1 egg
¾ cup milk

1 Preheat oven to 175°C (350°F).
2 Grease 20 cm x 10 cm (8" x 4") loaf tin.
3 Melt together butter and golden syrup and allow to cool.
4 Sift together dry ingredients, add sugar and prunes and mix thoroughly.
5 Beat egg and milk together.
6 Add egg and golden syrup mixtures to flour mixture and mix well.
7 Place in prepared tins and bake for approximately 60 minutes.
8 Serve sliced and buttered.

Variation
For a sugar free alternative leave out the sugar and golden syrup and increase butter to 3 tablespoons.

Pumpkin muffins

(use as a scone) makes 12

Gluten Free
Sugar Free

1 cup rice flour (sifted)
¾ cup maize meal
1 tablespoon baking powder
¼ teaspoon each of nutmeg,
  cinnamon and salt

½ cup cooked, mashed pumpkin
¼ cup milk
½ cup melted, cooled butter
2 lightly beaten eggs

1 Preheat oven to 175°C (350°F).
2 Grease muffin tray.
3 Mix flours, baking powder and spices.
4 Make a well in flour mixture, add all other ingredients and mix well.
5 Pour into tray and bake for approximately 35 minutes.
6 Serve hot or cold, sliced and buttered.

Spicy apple muffins

(use as a scone)   makes 12

Sugar Free

1 cup oatmeal
⅔ cup rice flour
3 teaspoons baking powder
½ teaspoon salt (optional)
¾ cup milk

1 egg
¾ cup finely chopped apple
¼ teaspoon nutmeg
1 teaspoon cinnamon
2 tablespoons raw sugar (optional)

1 Preheat oven to 175°C (350°F).
2 Grease muffin tray.
3 Mix flours and baking powder.
4 Mix in remaining ingredients.
5 Pour into tray and bake for approximately 25 minutes.
6 Eat hot or cold, sliced and buttered.

Sweet millet muffins
(use as a scone)

1½ cups millet meal
1½ cups oatmeal or barley flour
1 tablespoon baking powder
1½ tablespoons melted butter
1 cup milk

2 eggs
¼ cup sultanas
¼ cup chopped apricots
¼ cup raw sugar (optional)

1 Preheat oven to 175°C (350°F).
2 Grease muffin tray.
3 Mix flours and baking powder thoroughly.
4 Add all other ingredients (except dried fruit) and beat well.
5 Add dried fruits and mix thoroughly.
6 Pour into tray and bake for approximately 20–30 minutes.
7 Serve buttered or with jam and cream.

Biscuits & Slices

Anzac biscuits
Makes 20

1 cup rolled oats
1 cup oatmeal
½ cup raw sugar
¾ cup desiccated coconut

1 tablespoon honey
125 g/4 ounces butter
½ teaspoon bicarbonate of soda
1 tablespoon boiling water

1 Preheat oven to 150°C (300°F).
2 Grease biscuit tray.
3 Mix oats, oatmeal, sugar and coconut in a large bowl.
4 Melt butter and honey together.
5 Mix soda with boiling water and add to the melted butter.
6 Add butter mixture to the dry ingredients.
7 Mix well.
8 Place tablespoons of mixture onto greased tray.
9 Bake for approximately 20 minutes.

Apple raisin clusters
Makes 30

⅔ cup melted butter
1 egg
1 teaspoon grated lemon rind
2 tablespoons lemon juice
1 cup oatmeal
½ cup loosely packed brown sugar
1 teaspoon baking powder

½ teaspoon salt (optional)
½ teaspoon mixed spice
1½ cups rye flakes
1 cup grated mild cheese
½ cup finely chopped raisins
1 cup finely chopped apple

1 Preheat oven to 190°C (375°F).
2 Grease biscuit tray.
3 Mix butter, egg, lemon juice and rind.
4 Add remaining ingredients and mix well.
5 Place teaspoons of mixture onto prepared tray.
6 Bake for 12–15 minutes.
7 Loosen on trays and allow to cool.
8 In warm weather store in the refrigerator.

Variation
For a sugar free alternative omit sugar, grate apple instead of chopping
and add an extra egg.

Carob coconut slice

Makes 20

½ cup oatmeal
½ cup rice flour (sifted)
1 teaspoon baking powder
⅓ cup castor sugar

1 cup coconut
3 tablespoons carob powder
125 g/4 ounces melted butter

1 Preheat oven to 175°C (350°F).
2 Grease 30 cm x 20 cm (12" x 8") slice tray.
3 Combine all ingredients and mix thoroughly.
4 Press firmly into prepared tray.
5 Bake for approximately 20–25 minutes.
6 While still warm, ice with carob icing and sprinkle with coconut.
7 When cold cut into squares.

Carrot cookies

Makes 30

125 g/4 ounces butter
¼ cup raw sugar
1 egg
½ teaspoon vanilla
1¼ cups oatmeal
1 teaspoon baking powder

½ teaspoon cinnamon
3 tablespoons chopped nuts
1 cup steamed, mashed carrot
2 tablespoons coconut
1 teaspoon orange rind (finely grated)

1 Preheat oven to 175°C (350°F).
2 Grease biscuit tray.
3 Cream butter and sugar.
4 Add egg and vanilla, beat well.
5 Add rest of ingredients and mix thoroughly.
6 Place teaspoons of mixture onto prepared tray.
7 Bake for approximately 15–20 minutes.

Variation
For a sugar free alternative omit sugar and increase carrot to 1½ cups.

Cheese and onion nibbles
Makes approximately 40

1 cup oatmeal
½ cup sesame seeds
½ cup finely chopped onion

1½ cups cheddar or Colby cheese
  (grated)
⅔ cup water
pepper and salt (optional) to taste

1 Preheat oven to 180°C (360°F).
2 Grease biscuit tray.
3 Combine all ingredients in large bowl and mix well.
4 Place teaspoons of mixture onto prepared trays.
5 Bake for 5 minutes, then flatten biscuits slightly with a fork.
6 Return biscuits to oven for a further 10–15 minutes, or until crisp.
7 Loosen from tray while warm.
8 Remove from tray when cool.

Chocolate chip macaroons
Makes 12

1 cup corn flakes
½ cup icing sugar
1 egg white

½ teaspoon vanilla
½ cup coconut
60 g/2 ounces chocolate bits

1 Preheat oven to 175°C (350°F).
2 Grease biscuit tray.
3 Beat egg white until firm.
4 Gradually add sugar and beat until stiff.
5 Add remaining ingredients and stir well.
6 Place teaspoons of mixture onto greased tray.
7 Bake for approximately 10 minutes.

Chocolate crunch
Makes 20

2 cups rice crispies or puffs
½ cup barley flour or oatmeal
½–⅔ cup sugar (depending on taste)

2 cups desiccated coconut
250 g/8 ounces melted butter
3 tablespoons cocoa

1 Preheat oven to 175°C (350°F).
2 Grease 20 cm x 30 cm (8" x 12") slice tray.
3 Combine all ingredients, mix well.
4 Press into prepared tray.
5 Bake for 20–25 minutes.
6 Cut into squares while hot.
7 Remove from tray when completely cold.

Coconut cookies

Makes 30

125 g/4 ounces butter
½ cup lightly packed brown sugar
1 egg
1 teaspoon vanilla

1 cup rolled oats
½ cup chopped nuts
1 cup desiccated coconut

1 Preheat oven to 175°C (350°F).
2 Grease biscuit tray.
3 Cream butter and sugar until light and creamy.
4 Add egg and vanilla, beat well.
5 Stir in oats, nuts and coconut.
6 Drop teaspoons of mixture onto prepared tray.
7 Bake for approximately 10 minutes.
8 Remove from oven and press cookies flatter with the back of a spoon.
9 Bake for another 5 minutes.
10 Loosen on tray and leave until *completely cold*.

Variations
You could substitute barley flakes or rye flakes for the rolled oats.
For a gluten free alternative substitute soy flakes for the rolled oats.

Coconut crunchies

Makes 20

½ cup brown sugar
1 cup desiccated coconut
1 cup rolled oats

1¼ cups rice crispies or puffs
125 g/4 ounces butter
1 tablespoon honey

1 Preheat oven to 160°C (325°F).
2 Grease 20 cm x 30 cm (8" x 12") tray.
3 Mix sugar, coconut, rolled oats and rice bubbles.
4 Melt butter and honey, stir into dry ingredients.
5 Press into prepared tray.
6 Bake for approximately 25 minutes.
7 Cut into bars while still hot.
8 Remove when cool.

Variation
For a gluten free alternative substitute soy flakes for the rolled oats.

Coconut macaroons
Makes 12

¾ cup castor sugar
3 tablespoons ground rice
1 cup coconut

grated lemon rind
2 eggs whites (stiffly beaten)

1 Preheat oven to 175°C (350°F).
2 Grease baking tray.
3 Sift sugar and ground rice.
4 Add coconut and lemon rind.
5 Add stiffly beaten egg whites and mix well.
6 Drop tablespoons of mixture onto greased tray.
7 Bake for approximately 20 minutes.

Corny cheese biscuits
Makes 20

125 g/4 ounces butter
90 g/3 ounces cheddar cheese
½ teaspoon salt
¼ teaspoon cayenne
½ cup barley flour

½ cup rice flour
1 cup crushed corn flakes
2 eggs
1 tablespoon milk

1 Preheat oven to 175°C (350°F).
2 Lightly grease biscuit trays.
3 Cream butter.
4 Add grated cheese, salt, cayenne, flour and corn flakes.
5 Combine beaten egg and milk.
6 Add egg and milk to cheese mixture and mix thoroughly.
7 Roll teaspoons of mixture into balls.
8 Place on prepared trays about 5 cm (2") apart.
9 Press flat.
10 Bake for approximately 10 minutes.

Note: These biscuits will need to be kept in the refrigerator in warm weather. Remember to use sugarless corn flakes from a health food store.

Cottage cheese fingers
Makes 20

½ cup skim milk powder
½ cup water
1 cup barley flakes
1 cup desiccated coconut
½ cup chopped dates

⅓ cup orange juice
½ cup chopped nuts
½ cup cottage cheese
¼ cup raw sugar (optional)

1 Preheat oven to 180°C (360°F).
2 Grease 30 cm x 20 cm (12" x 8") tray.
3 Dissolve skim milk in the water.
4 Combine all ingredients in large bowl, mix well.
5 Press into prepared tray.
6 Bake for 30 minutes or until golden in colour.
7 Cut into fingers while still hot.
8 Remove from tray when completely cold.
Note: These are very moist cookies and will need to be eaten within two days. In hot weather store in the refrigerator.

Variations
Substitute rye flakes or rolled oats for the barley flakes.
For a gluten free alternative substitute soy flakes for the barley flakes.
For a sugar free alternative omit sugar.

Currant flake bars
Makes 20

125 g/4 ounces butter
1 tablespoon honey
1 cup crushed corn flakes
1 cup rye flakes

1 cup coconut
½ cup raw sugar
½ cup currants

1 Preheat oven to 175°C (350°F).
2 Grease a 20 cm x 30 cm (8" x 12") tray.
3 Place butter, honey and flakes in saucepan.
4 Stir continuously over low heat until well mixed.
5 Add remaining ingredients and mix well.
6 Press into prepared tray.
7 Bake for approximately 15 minutes.
8 Cut into bars while still warm.
9 Remove when cool.

Date and rice puff slice

Makes 20

125 g/4 ounces butter
1 cup brown sugar
pinch salt

1 cup chopped dates
1 teaspoon vanilla
4 cups rice puffs or krispies

1 Grease 20 cm x 30 cm (8" x 12") tray.
2 Place butter, sugar, salt, dates and vanilla in saucepan.
3 Simmer over low heat for 5 minutes.
4 Place rice bubbles in mixing bowl.
5 Pour butter mixture over rice bubbles and mix well.
6 Spread into greased tray.
7 Place in refrigerator until set.
8 Cut into squares when cold

Date crunchies

Makes 30

½ cup honey
½ cup vegetable oil
30 g/1 ounce butter
2 tablespoons peanut butter
2 tablespoons brown sugar
2 cups rye flakes

½ cup desiccated coconut
¼ cup skim milk powder or substitute
1 cup chopped nuts
1 cup sultanas
¾ cup chopped dates
1 egg

1 Preheat oven to 175°C (350°F).
2 Grease biscuit trays.
3 Place honey, oil, butter, peanut butter and brown sugar in saucepan.
4 Stir until butter has melted.
5 Mix in remaining ingredients.
6 Refrigerate mixture for 30 minutes.
7 Roll tablespoons of mixture into balls and place on prepared tray.
8 Bake for approximately 15–20 minutes.

Variations
Substitute barley flakes for rye flakes.
For a gluten free alternative substitute soy flour for rye flakes.

Fruit and nut slice
Makes 20

½ cup butter
¾ cup raw sugar
2 eggs
grated peel of an orange
1 tablespoon orange juice
1 cup rice flour (sifted)
¼ cup oatmeal

½ teaspoons baking powder
½ teaspoon cinnamon
½ teaspoon nutmeg
½ teaspoon ground cloves
¾ cup sultanas
¾ cup chopped nuts

1 Preheat oven to 175°C (350°F).
2 Grease 20 cm x 30 cm (12" x 8") slice tray.
3 Cream butter and sugar.
4 Beat in egg, orange juice and rind.
5 Mix together rice flour, oatmeal, baking powder and spices.
6 Blend into butter mixture.
7 Fold in nuts and sultanas.
8 Spread into prepared tray.
9 Bake for approximately 35 minutes.
10 Cool slightly, remove from tray.
11 Ice with a mixture of icing sugar and orange juice.
12 Cut into bars.

Honeyed corn flakes
Gluten Free
Makes 12

90 g/3 ounces butter or magarine
⅓ cup sugar

1 tablespoon honey
4 cups corn flakes.

1 Heat butter, sugar and honey until frothy.
2 Add corn flakes and mix well.
3 Spoon into patty cases.
4 Bake at 150°C (300°F) for 10 minutes.

Meringues
Makes 8

2 egg whites
125 g/4 ounces castor sugar

3 drops vanilla extract
½ level teaspoon baking powder

1 Preheat oven to 150°C (300°F).
2 Beat egg whites until stiff.
3 Divide sugar in half.
4 Beat mixture continuously while gradually adding one half of the sugar.
5 Fold in remaining sugar and baking powder.
6 Add vanilla.
7 Pipe or spoon onto oiled tray.
8 Bake for one to two hours until crisp on outside.

Variation
For hazelnut meringues, add 60 g/2 ounces of ground hazelnuts with the sugar and baking powder.

Muesli biscuits
Makes 30

1½ cups homemade muesli (see recipe
   page 84)
1½ cups barley flour
1 teaspoon cinnamon

125 g/4 ounces melted butter
2 eggs
4 tablespoons honey

1 Preheat oven to 175°C (350°F).
2 Grease biscuit tray.
3 Mix all dry ingredients.
4 Add melted butter and beaten eggs.
5 Add honey and mix thoroughly.
6 Drop teaspoons of mixture onto prepared tray.
7 Bake for 12–15 minutes.

Variation
For a sugar free alternative omit honey.

No-bake cookies

Makes 30

4 cups corn flakes
3 tablespoons cocoa
1 cup chopped mixed dried fruits (eg
sultanas, currants, raisins)

1 cup icing sugar (sifted)
½ cup chopped mixed nuts
¾ cup melted butter

1 Combine all ingredients, add butter and mix thoroughly.
2 Spoon into paper patty cups.
3 Chill.

Nutty oat slice

Makes 20

125 g/4 ounces butter
2 cups rolled oats
½ cup brown sugar

½ cup chopped nuts
½ cup coconut
1 egg (optional)

1 Preheat oven to 175°C (350°F).
2 Grease 30 cm x 20 cm (12" x 8") slice tray.
3 Melt butter.
4 Combine all other ingredients in a bowl.
5 Pour melted butter over, mix thoroughly.
6 Bake for approximately 20 minutes.
7 Cool slightly then slice.

Variations
Use barley flakes or rye flakes instead of rolled oats. Sunflower seeds
can be substituted for all or part of the nuts.
For a gluten free alternative substitute soy flakes for the rolled oats.

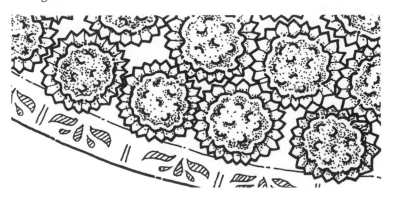

Oat crisps
Makes 30

125 g/4 ounces butter
½ cup brown sugar
½ teaspoon vanilla
¼ teaspoon salt (optional)

½ teaspoon bicarbonate of soda
1 cup oatmeal
1 cup rolled oats
¼ cup coconut

1 Preheat oven to 175°C (350°F).
2 Grease biscuit tray.
3 Cream butter, sugar and vanilla.
4 Mix in oatmeal, salt and bicarbonate of soda, then oats and coconut, mix well.
5 Roll into small balls.
6 Place on prepared tray.
7 Bake for approximately 15 minutes.

Variation
Swirl ½ teaspoon chocolate icing on centre of each biscuit and top with a nut or sandwich two biscuits together with chocolate icing.

Oatmeal cookies
Makes 20

⅓ cup butter
½ cup brown sugar
1 egg
¾ cup rice flour (sifted)
½ teaspoon vanilla extract

1 cup oatmeal
¼ teaspoon bicarbonate of soda
¼ teaspoon salt (optional)
½ teaspoon cinnamon
¼ teaspoon nutmeg

1 Preheat oven to 175°C (350°F).
2 Grease biscuit tray.
3 Cream butter and sugar.
4 Add egg, vanilla and beat well.
5 Add remaining ingredients and mix thoroughly.
6 Place teaspoons of mixture on prepared tray.
7 Bake for approximately 15–20 minutes.

Variation
For banana cookies, add ½ cup mashed banana; for sugarless banana cookies leave out sugar and add ¾ cup mashed banana; for ginger cookies add 1½ teaspoons of dried ginger to basic oatmeal cookies.

Pineapple yoghurt slice

Makes 12

Base

2 cups rolled oats
¾ cup dates

60 g/2 ounces melted butter

1 Preheat oven to 175°C (350°F).
2 Grease 28 cm x 18 cm (11" x 7") high-sided tin.
3 Blend rolled oats and dates in a food processor or blender.
4 Gradually add melted butter while food processor is still on.
5 Press into prepared tin.
6 Bake for approximately 7–9 minutes.
7 Cool while preparing topping.

Topping

1 tablespoon gelatine
2 tablespoons water
1½ cups natural yoghurt
2 tablespoons honey

1 cup pineapple (pulped)
2 egg whites
2 bananas

1 Sprinkle gelatine over water, dissolve over simmering water, cool slightly.
2 Combine yoghurt and honey.
3 Add dissolved gelatine and passionfruit pulp, combine well.
4 Beat egg whites until stiff, fold into yoghurt mixture.
5 Arrange thinly sliced bananas over prepared base.
6 Spread yoghurt mixture over and smooth top.
7 Refrigerate until set.
8 Cut into slices.

Variation

For a gluten-free variation use base of strawberry yoghurt slice (see recipe page 44).

Pineapple cheese fingers
Makes 30

1 cup brown rice flakes (or soy flakes)
1 cup desiccated coconut
2/3 cup chopped dried pineapple
1/2 cup cottage cheese

1/2 cup skim milk powder dissolved in 2/3–3/4 cup unsweetened pineapple juice
1/2 cup sunflower seeds (or chopped nuts)

1 Preheat oven to 180°C (360°F).
2 Grease 30 cm x 20 cm (12" x 8") tray.
3 Combine all ingredients in large bowl and mix well.
4 Press into prepared tray.
5 Bake for 20–30 minutes until crisp.
6 Cut into fingers while still hot.
7 Remove from tray when completely cold.

Variations (using gluten grains)
Substitute rye flakes, rolled oats or barley flakes for the rice flakes. Please remember rye, oats and barley contain gluten.

Rye flake cookies
Makes 30

1 cup oatmeal
1 cup coconut
1 cup rye flakes
1/2–1 cup raw sugar (depending on personal preference)

125 g/4 ounces butter
2 tablespoons water
1 tablespoon honey
1 teaspoon bicarbonate of soda

1 Preheat oven to 175°C (350°F).
2 Grease biscuit tray.
3 Combine oatmeal, coconut, rye flakes and sugar in a large basin.
4 Place butter, water and honey in a saucepan and bring to the boil.
5 When boiling, add 1 teaspoon bicarbonate of soda.
6 Pour contents of saucepan onto dry ingredients and mix well.
7 Roll into balls and place on prepared tray.
8 Bake for approximately 12–15 minutes.

Savoury rye crackers

Sugar Free

Makes 20

²/₃ cup rye flour   *½ cup water*
1¼ cups rice flour   *salt to taste*
4 tablespoons oil

1 Preheat oven to 160°C (325°F).
2 Lightly oil a biscuit tray.
3 Mix flours and salt.
4 Add water and oil and mix well.
5 Knead until smooth, for approximately 5 minutes.
6 Roll as thinly as possible (3 mm).
7 Cut into shapes (squares, rectangles, circles or triangles).
8 Place on biscuit tray.
9 Prick all over with a fork.
10 Sprinkle with a little extra salt.
11 Bake for 15–20 minutes.

Variation
Instead of salt use garlic salt, steak spice, parmesan cheese, etc.

Slice with apple

Sugar Free

Base

2 cups rolled oats   *60 g/2 ounces melted butter*
¾ cup dates

1 Grease 28 cm x 18 cm (11" x 7") low-sided tray.
2 Blend rolled oats and dates in a food processor or blender.
3 Gradually add melted butter while food processor is still on.
4 Press into prepared tray.

Topping

6 cooking apples (4 large)   *¼ cup candied dried fruits, finely*
3-6 tablespoons water   *diced*
2 cloves   *flaked almonds*

1 Preheat oven to 175°C (350°F).
2 Peel, core and slice apples.
3 Place all ingredients except almonds in a saucepan.
4 Simmer gently until apples are tender.
5 Remove cloves and spread topping over prepared base.
6 Cover liberally with flaked almonds.
7 Bake until almonds are golden brown, approximately 30 minutes.
8 Cool and refrigerate.
9 Cut into slices.

Strawberry yoghurt slice
Makes 12

Base

1½ cups crushed corn flakes
½ cup desiccated coconut
125 g/4 ounces butter

1 tablespoon sugar
1 tablespoon milk

1 Grease a 28 cm x 18 cm (11" x 7") low-sided tray.
2 Put corn flakes and coconut in large bowl.
3 Mix remaining ingredients in saucepan.
4 Stir over low heat until melted and thoroughly mixed.
5 Pour over dry ingredients, mix well.
6 Press into prepared tray.
7 Store in refrigerator while making the topping.

Topping

1 tablespoon gelatine
¼ cup water
½ pint strawberries, finely chopped,
    with stems removed
¼ cup sugar
¼ cup strawberry jam

¾ cup strawberry flavoured yoghurt
125 g/4 ounces cream cheese
1 tablespoon honey
1 teaspoon each of lemon juice and
    grated lemon rind

1 Sprinkle gelatine over water to soften.
2 In a saucepan combine strawberries, sugar, softened gelatine and strawberry jam.
3 Bring to the boil, stirring until sugar and gelatine have dissolved thoroughly.
4 Set aside to cool.
5 Cream yoghurt, cheese and honey together.
6 Add lemon juice and rind.
7 Stir into the creamed cheese and yoghurt mixture.
8 Spread over corn flake base.
9 Return to refrigerator until properly set, possibly overnight.
10 Cut into slices or squares.

Variation

For a sugar free, gluten free alternative: **Base.** Leave out sugar, use sugarless corn flakes from health food store, and increase milk to 1½ tablespoons. **Topping.** Leave out honey and sugar, use sugarless jam (homemade or commercial carbohydrate modified), increase jam to ⅓ cup and use plain yoghurt.

For a low fat alternative use smooth ricotta in place of cream cheese and use low fat yoghurt.

Shortbread

Barley shortbread

¼ *cup soy flour*
1 cup rice flour
1½ cups barley flour

250 g/8 ounces butter
*⅓–½ cup castor sugar (according to
    taste)*

1 Preheat oven to 150°C (300°F).
2 Grease two biscuit trays.
3 Sift flours together.
4 Beat butter and sugar together until light and creamy.
5 Gradually add flours and mix to a firm dough.
6 Divide dough into four and form into balls.
7 Roll each ball between two sheets of plastic wrap, to a thickness of
    approximately 1 cm and until circular in shape.
8 Decorate edge by pinching between fingers.
9 Prick all over with a fork.
10 Mark into 8 triangles (see diagram) with a knife.
11 Bake for approximately 40 minutes.

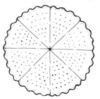

Rye shortbread

1¼ cups rice flour
½ cup soy flour
1½ cups rye flour

250 g/8 ounces butter
½ cup castor sugar

1 Preheat oven to 150°C (300°F).
2 Grease two biscuit trays.
3 Sift flours together.
4 Beat butter and sugar together until light and creamy.
5 Gradually add flours and mix to a firm dough.
6 Divide dough into four and form into balls.
7 Roll each ball between two sheets of plastic wrap, to a thickness of
    approximately 1 cm and until circular in shape.
8 Decorate edge by pinching between fingers.
9 Prick all over with a fork.
10 Mark into 8 triangles (see diagram) with a knife.
11 Bake for approximately 50 minutes.

Bread

An acceptable 'wheatless bread' proved to be one of the most difficult things to achieve. It wasn't until I set aside all the basic 'laws' of good breadmaking that I started to have success. In the course of my experimenting I used instant yeast, sour-dough yeast and baking powder in an effort to achieve the desired result. Each method had its own advantages, and because of this I have included all methods in the various recipes.

The sour-dough yeast method is especially rewarding, even though it does require a lot more work. The subtleness of the yeast allows the taste of the flours to be appreciated.

The breads using baking powder are very quick and easy to prepare. They are of great benefit when you haven't got time to make a yeasted bread. Since starting this book, I have also found out that a lot of people have a combined wheat-yeast allergy. These people in particular will find the breads using baking powder useful.

If you need to make a gluten-free bread, I suggest you buy one of the commercially-produced gluten free bread mixes. These are available at health food stores and some supermarkets. For added interest and nutrition you might be able to add some unhulled millet, flax seed, linseed, or sesame seed. I have not tried this myself, but I feel it should not be detrimental to the finished loaf. Please remember that the gluten free bread mixes are processed from wheat flour and should not be used by anyone with a wheat allergy.

I have also included a few recipes using breadcrumbs in the dessert section of this book. When you have gone to all the trouble to make your own bread, you certainly don't feel like throwing it out, even if it is stale. So if your bread is too stale to enjoy, recycle it as a delicious dessert! Or make it into breadcrumbs and store it in the freezer to use for coating chicken pieces, schnitzel etc.

Hint: If you do need a breadcrumb coating and you don't have any wheatless breadcrumbs, use crushed corn flakes.

Corn bread

1 cup corn meal (polenta)
1/3 cup soy flour
1/4 cup oatmeal
3 teaspoons baking powder

1/2 teaspoon salt
1 egg
1–1 1/4 cup milk
1/4 cup skim milk powder (dissolved
in the cup of milk)

1 Preheat oven to 190°C (375°F).
2 Grease 20 cm x 10 cm (8" x 4") loaf tin.
3 Mix dry ingredients.
4 Add milk and egg, mix until smooth.
5 Pour into prepared tin and bake for approximately 30 minutes.
6 Can be eaten hot or cold or toasted.

Variations

For a lighter texture fold in two stiffly beaten egg whites just before baking (use yolks in place of the egg in recipe).

Add 4 tablespoons grated medium cheddar or Colby cheese and/or 1/2 cup thinly sliced celery.

When cooked, top with grated medium cheddar or Colby cheese and place under griller, or return to oven until cheese melts.

Opposite: breads. In a clockwise direction from the bottom of the page: cornbread, rye bread (yeastless), sour dough barley bread, rice and oat muffins and spicy fruit bread.

Overleaf: breakfast foods. From left to right: roasted muesli, rice and oat muffins, millet muffins and sour dough raisin bread.

Cottage cheese & herb bread

Sugar Free

2 rounded teaspoons instant yeast
¾ cup lukewarm water
1 cup rice flour
¾ cup creamed cottage cheese
1 egg

1 tablespoon chopped chives
1 tablespoon sugar, optional
½ tablespoon dried Italian seasoning
1½ cups oatmeal
1 teaspoon salt

1 Grease a 20 cm x 10 cm (8" x 4") loaf tin.
2 Mix together yeast and water.
3 In a large bowl combine rice flour, cheese, egg, chives, salt, sugar and seasoning, add yeast mixture, beat with a wooden spoon until well combined.
4 Stir in oatmeal ½ cup at a time, beat well.
5 Cover and stand in a warm position for 1–1½ hours or until dough has almost doubled in size.
6 Stir down with a wooden spoon and place in a greased loaf tin.
7 Cover and stand for approximately 30 minutes.
8 Bake at 175°C (350°F) for approximately 45 minutes.

Variations
For a yeastless bread use 3 teaspoons baking powder, leave out steps 2, 5, 6 and 7, pour into prepared loaf tin and bake as above.
For a lighter texture use 2 egg yolks in bread mixture, in place of the one egg. Mix in 2 stiffly beaten egg whites just before baking.

Opposite: desserts. In a clockwise direction from the top of the page: apricot shortcake, chocolate pudding, apple pie (sweet barley pastry), apricot shortcake and sago plum pudding.

Overleaf: main meals. From left to right: family pastie with potato pastry and pizza.

Rice and oat muffins
(bread rolls substitute)
Makes 12

1 cup oatmeal	*½ teaspoon salt*
⅔ cup rice flour (sifted)	*¾ cup milk*
3 teaspoons baking powder	*1 egg*

1 Preheat oven to 175°C (350°F).
2 Grease muffin tray.
3 Mix flours, baking powder and salt.
4 Mix in remaining ingredients.
5 Pour into tray and bake for approximately 25 minutes.
6 Cut muffins in half, butter and spread with desired topping.

Variations

For a multi-grain variation add 2 tablespoons of each of the following: unroasted buckwheat; unhulled millet; chopped sunflower seeds; flax seed.

For cheese, onion and bacon muffins place an onion ring on each muffin, sprinkle generously with grated cheese and top with chopped bacon pieces. Bake as above.

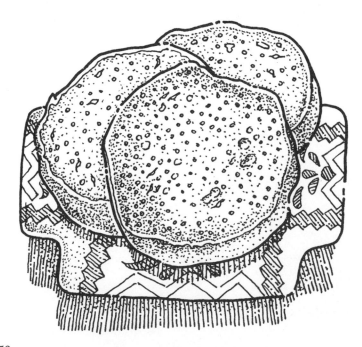

Savoury millet muffins

(bread rolls substitute)
Makes 12

1½ cups millet flour
1½ cups barley flour or oatmeal
1¼ tablespoons baking powder

1 cup milk
2 eggs
1½ tablespoons melted butter

1 Preheat oven to 175°C (350°F).
2 Grease muffin tray.
3 Mix flours and baking powder thoroughly.
4 Lightly beat eggs and milk.
5 Add to flour mixture.
6 Beat in butter.
7 Bake for 20–30 minutes.
8 Cut muffins in half, butter and spread with desired topping.

Sour cream raisin bread

3 tablespoons oil
2 tablespoons honey
3 eggs
1 cup rice flour (sifted)
1 cup oatmeal
1 teaspoon salt

3 teaspoons baking powder
2 teaspoons cinnamon
½ teaspoon nutmeg
1 cup sour cream
1 cup raisins

1 Preheat oven to 175°C (350°F).
2 Grease 20 cm x 10 cm (8" x 4") loaf tin.
3 Beat together oil and honey, add eggs and beat well.
4 Mix together flours, salt, baking powder, cinnamon and nutmeg.
5 Gradually add flour mixture to egg mixture, mix well.
6 Add sour cream and raisins, mix well.
7 Pour into prepared loaf tin.
8 Bake for approximately 40–45 minutes.
9 Allow to cool for 5 minutes before removing to rack.

Variation
For a sugar free alternative omit honey.

Sour-dough barley bread

1 tablespoon oil　　　　　　*1 cup sour dough yeast*
3 cups barley flour　　　　　*⅔ cup water*

Use method as for sour dough rye bread (see recipe below). The
barley bread dough will need more kneading (approximately 15 minutes each time). It will not rise as high as the rye bread and must be
baked at a lower temperature, 175°C (350°F). Bake for 70 minutes
covered with foil and 10 minutes uncovered.

Multigrain Variation
Add any combination of the following wholegrains: unroasted buckwheat; flax seed; millet; linseed; chopped nuts/seeds.

Sour-dough rye bread

1 tablespoon oil　　　　　　*1 cup sour-dough yeast*
1 cup rye flour　　　　　　　*⅔ cup water*
2 cups rice flour plus approximately
　½ cup extra for kneading

1　Oil a 20 cm x 10 cm (8" x 4") loaf tin.
2　Combine all ingredients and knead until dough becomes too sticky
　to handle (2–3 minutes).
3　Put dough in oiled bowl, cover and place in a warm position.
4　Let dough rise until it increases itself by half (2–4 hours).
5　Using rice flour, add to the dough as much flour as necessary to
　be just able to handle it. The dough will be quite sticky so oil your
　hands if necessary.
6　Knead for approximately 5 minutes.
7　Shape dough to fit into loaf tin.
8　Place in a warm position (as above) and let dough rise until the
　centre of the loaf has risen above the height of the tin. The dough
　will just comfortably fit the loaf tin, do not expect it to rise too
　much.
9　Preheat oven to 200°C (400°F).
10　Cover loaf loosely with aluminium foil and secure edges by pinch-
　ing onto rim of loaf tin.
11　Bake for approximately 60 minutes.
12　Remove foil for the last 10 minutes if a crisper crust is required.
13　Remove from tin and allow to cool before cutting.

Sour-dough yeast

2 cups warm water
1 tablespoon dry active yeast
1 teaspoon sugar

1 cup rice flour
1 cup barley flour

1 Mix all ingredients together and cover with a loose cloth.
2 Stand in a warm position until mixture bubbles (approximately 30 minutes).
3 Store in the fridge until needed (do not use for 24 hours).
4 Whenever you use yeast, replace each cupful used with ½ cup each of rice and barley flours, 1 cup water and 1 teaspoon sugar.
5 Let stand in a warm position again until mixture bubbles.
6 Store in fridge but do not use for 24 hours.

Spicy fruit bread

1 quantity of yeastless barley bread
  (see recipe above)
200 g/6½ ounces chopped dried fruit

½ teaspoon nutmeg
2 teaspoons cinnamon
2 tablespoons brown sugar

1 Add above ingredients to the barley bread before the water and oil.
2 Proceed as for barley bread (see page 52).

Variation
For a sugar free alternative omit sugar.

Yeastless barley bread

Sugar Free

1½ cups barley flour
1½ cups rice flour
2 teaspoons oil

1½ cups water
6 teaspoons baking powder

1 Oil a 20 cm x 10 cm (8" x 4") loaf tin.
2 Preheat oven to 175°C (350°F).
3 Combine sifted flours and baking powder.
4 Add water and oil.
5 Mix until well combined.
6 Place dough into oiled loaf tin.
7 Bake covered with foil for 65 minutes.
8 Remove foil and bake for a further 10 minutes if a crisper crust is required.

Yeastless rye bread

1 cup rye flour
1½ cups rice flour
½ cup soy flour
2 teaspoons oil

1½ cups water
6 teaspoons baking powder
1 tablespoon molasses (optional)

1 Preheat oven to 190°C (375°F).
2 Grease 20 cm x 10 cm (8" x 4") loaf tin.
3 Sift rice flour, soy flour and baking powder.
4 Add rye flour.
5 Add water, oil and molasses.
6 Mix until well combined.
7 Place mixture in prepared tin.
8 Cover with foil, leaving room for expansion.
9 Bake for approximately 70 minutes.
10 Remove foil for last 10 minutes if a crisper crust is required.

Variation
Add 1–2 tablespoons caraway seeds to dry ingredients. Sprinkle a little extra caraway seeds on top of loaf before baking.
For a sugar free alternative omit molasses.

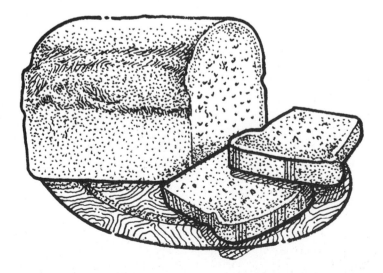

Pastry

Barley pastry

Makes enough to line and cover 20 cm (8") to 23 cm (9")
pie plate

1 cup barley flour
½ cup soy flour
½ cup rye flour

125 g/4 ounces butter
2 eggs
salt (optional)

1 Sift flours together.
2 Rub butter into flour.
3 Beat eggs together, add to flour and mix to a firm dough.
4 Knead lightly and use as required.
This is suitable for savoury pies, quiche, sweet pies and tarts.
Note: When rolling do not use flour. Place ball of dough between two sheets of plastic wrap and roll with rolling pin.

Variation
For sweet barley pastry add ⅓ cup sugar to flours.
For an egg free alternative substitute 60 g/2 ounces cottage cheese and enough water to obtain desired consistency.

Egg and bacon pie

1 quantity potato pastry
3 slices bacon, chopped
salt and pepper to taste

2 teaspoons finely chopped parsley
4 eggs, lightly beaten

1 Preheat oven 200°C (400°F).
2 Grease 23 cm (9") pie plate.
3 Divide pastry into two, then roll one piece to line prepared plate.
4 Combine filling ingredients and pour into pastry case.
5 Roll remaining pastry to cover the pie.
6 Trim edges, prick and glaze with milk.
7 Bake for approximately 40 minutes.

Variation
Use barley pastry (see recipe above) instead of potato pastry, but *please note barley pastry is not gluten free.*

Family meat pie

Gluten Free
Sugar Free

1 quantity of potato pastry
500 g/1 pound minced beef
1 large onion, diced

2 beef stock cubes
¼ cup water
2 tablespoons pure maize corn flour

1 Place filling ingredients, except corn flour, in a large saucepan.
2 Simmer gently until meat is cooked, approximately 30 minutes.
3 Add corn flour and stir until mixture thickens.
4 Preheat oven to 200°C (400°F).
5 Grease 23 cm (9") pie plate.
6 Roll half the pastry to line the base of prepared pie plate.
7 Place filling in pastry case.
8 Roll remaining pastry to cover pie.
9 Trim edges, make slits in top of pie.
10 Glaze with milk and bake for approximately 30 minutes.

Variations
Use rye pastry (see recipe page 60) instead of potato pastry, but *please note rye pastry is not gluten free.*

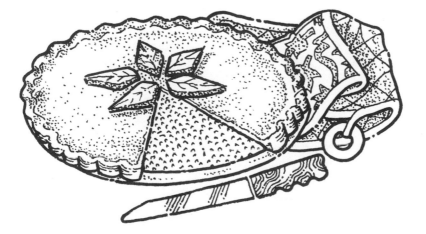

Family pastie

1 quantity of potato pastry (see recipe
   page 59)
250 g/8 ounces finely minced beef
1 onion, diced
1 large carrot, diced
1 potato, diced

½ cup peas or beans
1 beef stock cube
salt and pepper to taste
¼ cup water
1–2 tablespoons of pure maize corn
   flour

1 Combine filling ingredients, except corn flour, and simmer gently until cooked, approximately 30 minutes.
2 Add corn flour and stir until mixture thickens.
3 Allow to cool.
4 Preheat oven to 200°C (400°F).
5 Grease 23 cm (9") pie plate.
6 Roll half the pastry to line the base of prepared pie plate.
7 Place filling in pastry case.
8 Roll remaining pastry to cover pastie.
9 Trim edges, make slits in top of pastie.
10 Glaze with milk and bake for approximately 30 minutes.

Variation
Use rye pastry (see recipe page 60) instead of potato pastry, but *please note the rye pastry is not gluten free.*

Potato pastry

Gluten Free
Sugar Free

*Makes enough to line and cover 20 cm (8") to 23 cm (9")
pie plate*

1 egg
2 tablespoons water
1½ cups mashed potato (see below)

1¼ cups pure maize corn flour
½ cup powdered milk
salt and pepper to taste

1 Combine egg and water with potatoes and mix well.
2 Combine flour, powdered milk, salt and pepper.
3 Stir into potato mixture, knead lightly.
4 Roll pastry between two pieces of clear plastic wrap to required size
   (base and cover), then remove plastic.
5 Pour in desired, pre-cooked filling.
6 Cover with remaining pastry, prick and glaze with milk.
7 Bake at 200°C (400°F) for 20–30 minutes.
Note: If using a very moist filling pre-cook pie shell for 15 minutes.
(Mashed Potato: potatoes must be steamed, and then mashed without
adding any liquid or butter during the mashing.)

Quiche Lorraine

Sugar Free

Serves 6

*½ quantity rye or barley pastry (see
   recipes pages 56 and 60)*
6 green onions, chopped
2 slices bacon, chopped

½ cup warm milk
3 eggs, beaten
½ teaspoon salt
*½ cup grated medium cheddar or
   Colby cheese*

1 Preheat oven to 200°C (400°F).
2 Line greased 23 cm (9") pie plate with pastry.
3 Combine remaining ingredients and pour into pastry case.
4 Bake at 200°C (400°F) for 40 minutes.

Rye pastry

*Makes enough to line and cover 20 cm (8") to 23 cm (9")
pie plate*

1 cup rye flour	*125 g/4 ounces butter*
½ cup rice flour	*2 eggs*
½ cup soy flour	*salt (optional)*

1 Sift flours together.
2 Rub butter into flours until mixture resembles breadcrumbs.
3 Beat eggs together, add to flour and mix to a firm dough.
4 Knead lightly and use as required.
This is suitable for savoury pies or quiches.
Note: When rolling do not use flour. Place ball of dough between two
sheets of plastic wrap and roll. It makes handling a lot easier.

Variation
For an egg free alternative substitute 60 g/2 ounces cottage cheese and
enough water to obtain desired consistency.

Main Meals

Aussie quiche

Serves 6

Crust

2 teaspoons yeast extract or 2 beef
    stock cubes
2½ cups hot water
¾ cup rice

1 egg, lightly beaten
½ cup grated medium cheddar or
    Colby cheese
2 teaspoons pure maize corn flour

1 Preheat oven to 175°C (350°F).
2 Grease 23 cm (9") pie plate.
3 Dissolve yeast extract or cubes in water.
4 Cook rice in stock until tender and liquid is absorbed.
5 Allow rice to cool and add egg, cheese, flour and mix well.
6 Press rice mixture into pie plate.
7 Cool for 20 minutes.

Filling

½ cup chopped ham
1 medium zucchini, sliced
1 tomato, sliced
½ cup sliced fresh mushrooms
1 cup finely grated medium cheddar or
    Colby cheese

3 eggs, lightly beaten
½ cup cream
½ cup milk
pinch of salt, pinch of pepper

1 Place ham, mushrooms and ¾ cheese into crust.
2 Whisk together eggs, cream, milk and seasonings and pour slowly into crust.
3 Arrange zucchini around edge of plate.
4 Garnish with tomato and remaining cheese.
5 Bake in moderate oven for 45 minutes.

Published with permission of
The Rice Marketing Board

Buckwheat spaghetti

½ cup buckwheat flour
2 teaspoons oil

2 tablespoons water

1 Combine all ingredients, to form a firm dough.
2 Knead for 10 minutes.
3 Place dough on an oiled tray and roll as *thinly* as possible.
4 Slice into fine strips (wide ones do not cook properly).
5 Bring to the boil plenty of salted water with 2 teaspoons of oil added.
6 Boil spaghetti for 3 minutes.
7 Drain and serve with a topping of your choice.

Pizza base

Makes 2 x 28 cm (11") pizza bases

1 cup rye flour
1½ cups rice flour
⅔ cup soy flour
3 teaspoons baking powder

salt to taste
7 tablespoons oil
1 cup milk

1 Preheat oven to 175°C (350°F).
2 Sift flours, salt and baking powder into a large bowl.
3 Add milk and oil, mix well.
4 Knead until smooth (approximately 10 minutes).
5 Roll out onto oiled pizza trays.
6 Top with your favourite toppings (see below).
7 Bake for 10 minutes at 175°C (350°F), then another 10 minutes at 200°C (400°F).
8 Serve hot or freeze and reheat when needed.

Suggested toppings

First spread the pizza base with tomato paste or tomato sauce. Then cover thickly with grated cheese, and any selection of the following: sliced tomato; strips of salami; onion rings; crushed, drained pineapple; chopped ham or bacon; small prawns (cooked); sliced olives; sliced anchovy; champignons; lightly beaten egg in centre; season to taste and sprinkle lightly with oregano.

Potato pancakes
Makes 12

250 g/8 ounces cooked mashed potato   *¼ teaspoon salt*
  (still warm), see below   *1 tablespoon butter*
3 tablespoons pure maize corn flour

1 Cream butter and slowly add potato.
2 Add salt and flour to make a soft, dry consistency.
3 Knead lightly on floured surface and roll as thin as required.
4 Cut into circles using the rim of a cup or glass, then prick all over.
5 Shallow fry for 2–3 minutes each side.
6 Eat hot with tomato sauce, or use as a side dish. Can be eaten cold spread with butter.

(Mashed potato: potatoes should be steamed, and then mashed without adding any liquid or butter during the mashing.)

Stuffing

1 chopped onion   *2 eggs*
2 cups rolled oats (or wheatless   *chopped parsley*
  breadcrumbs)   *pepper and salt to taste*
1 teaspoon Italian seasoning

1 Fry onion lightly in a little butter.
2 Mix all ingredients together.
3 Use as desired.

Eggless stuffing

1 chopped onion   *chopped parsley*
2 cups rolled oats (or wheatless   *2 tablespoons butter or substitute*
  breadcrumbs)   *¼ cup milk*
1 teaspoon Italian seasoning   *salt and pepper to taste*

1 Fry onion lightly in a little of the butter.
2 Add remaining ingredients, stir over heat until butter has melted.
3 Use as desired.

Sweet corn & potato patties

Gluten Free
(only if using
crushed
corn flakes)
Sugar Free

1 egg
1 tablespoon milk
1½ cups cooked corn kernels (canned,
  fresh or frozen)

2 cups mashed potato (still warm)
salt and pepper to taste
crushed corn flakes or wheatless
  breadcrumbs for coating

1 Mix egg and milk
2 Add remaining ingredients, except corn flakes or breadcrumbs.
3 Stand mixture for 15 minutes.
4 Form into patties.
5 Roll in breadcrumbs.
6 Shallow fry in oil or butter.

Note: Remember to use sugarless corn flakes from a health food store.
(Mashed potato: potatoes should be steamed and then mashed without
adding any liquid or butter during the mashing.)

Sweet corn patties

Sugar Free

Makes 30

1 cup buckwheat flour
1 cup rice flour or corn meal
1 egg
1¾ cups milk

2 teaspoons curry powder
black pepper
1 large chopped onion
1½ cups cooked corn

1 Mix flours.
2 Add ½ milk and egg, beat well.
3 Add remaining ingredients, mix thoroughly.
4 Heat oil or ghee in frypan then drop in tablespoons of mixture and
   fry.
5 Flip over and fry on other side.

Vegetable patties
Makes 20

1 cup leftover vegetables
1 egg
1 chopped onion
½ teaspoon mixed herbs

1½ cups buckwheat flour
milk
black pepper and salt to taste
  (optional)

1 Mash vegetables.
2 Add remaining ingredients — mixture should resemble a thick pancake batter — and beat well.
3 Drop tablespoons of mixture into hot oil or butter.
4 Fry both sides.
5 Serve hot.

Wholemeal pancakes
Makes 6

1 cup buckwheat flour
1 cup corn meal (polenta)

1 egg
1¾ cups milk

1 Mix dry ingredients.
2 Add ½ milk and egg, stirring until smooth.
3 Beat well, then stir in remaining milk.
4 Pour required amount into hot oil or butter.
5 Fry one side, flip over and fry other side.
6 Serve hot and buttered, with topping of your choice.

Zucchini and corn bake

½ cup grated zucchini
440 g/14 ounces drained whole corn
  kernels
1 onion peeled and finely chopped
½ cup grated, peeled carrot
½ cup finely diced celery
1 cup finely chopped shallots

½ cup grated cheese
½ cup oatmeal or buckwheat flour
30 g/1 ounce melted butter
4 eggs
pepper to taste
salt to taste (optional)

1 Preheat oven to 175°C (350°F).
2 Combine all ingredients and mix well.
3 Grease a 20 cm (8") round cake tin.
4 Spoon mixture into tin.
5 Bake for 35–40 minutes.
6 Turn out and slice.

Desserts

Apple crumble tart

½ quantity barley pastry
3 cooking apples

1 tablespoon castor sugar
pinch cinnamon

1 Preheat oven to 200°C (400°F).
2 Roll pastry to line a greased 20 cm (8") pie plate.
3 Peel and slice apples finely (for best results use a vegetable peeler to slice apples).
4 Place a layer of sliced apple in uncooked pastry case.
5 Sprinkle with a little sugar and cinnamon.
6 Repeat until all apple, sugar and cinnamon are used.

Crumble Topping

½ teaspoon cinnamon
½ teaspoon nutmeg
¾ cup barley flour

¼ cup brown sugar
¼ cup butter, softened (not melted)

1 Combine all topping ingredients.
2 Rub together with finger tips until mixture resembles breadcrumbs.
3 Sprinkle over pie.
4 Bake for approximately 40 minutes.

Apple crunch
Serves 4

1 quantity of stewed apples (see recipe
   page 70)

Crunch Topping

½ cup oatmeal

1½ teaspoons cinnamon

3 tablespoons butter

½ cup raw sugar

1 Preheat oven to 175°C (350°F).
2 Put oatmeal and cinnamon in bowl.
3 Rub butter in with fingers until mixture is crumbly.
4 Add sugar and mix well.
5 Sprinkle over stewed apples.
6 Bake until top is crisp and lightly browned.
7 Serve hot or cold with cream or ice cream.

Apple pie

1 quantity sweet barley pastry (see
  recipe page 56)

7 cooking apples

½ teaspoon grated lemon rind

3 tablespoons sugar

¼ cup water

2 tablespoons apricot jam

1 Peel, quarter and core apples, cut each quarter in half lengthways.
2 Place in saucepan with water, sugar and lemon rind.
3 Cook covered until apples are almost tender and still holding their shape.
4 Remove from heat, drain and allow to cool.
5 Preheat oven to 200°C (400°F).
6 Roll ½ pastry to line base and sides of 23 cm (9") pie plate.
7 Spread base with apricot jam and cover with apples.
8 Roll remaining pastry to cover top of pie.
9 Trim, decorate and glaze with a little sugar and water.
10 Cut at least 3 slits in top of pie.
11 Bake for 20 minutes at 200°C, then for a further 20–25 minutes at 175°C (350°F).

Variations

For a sugar free alternative omit apricot jam, omit sugar from pastry
and apples and add 2 tablespoons of chopped dried apricots to apples
before cooking.

Use peaches or apricots.

Apple sponge

Stewed apples

6–8 cooking apples

½ cup raw sugar (optional)

4–8 tablespoons water

4 cloves

1 Peel, core and slice apples.
2 Place all ingredients in a saucepan.
3 Simmer gently until the apples are tender.
4 Place in a greased casserole.

Sponge topping:

1¼ cups rice flour (sifted)

½ cup soy flour (sifted)

3 teaspoons baking powder

½ cup castor sugar

125 g/4 ounces butter, melted

⅔ cup milk

2 eggs

1 teaspoon vanilla essence

1 Preheat oven to 175°C (350°F).
2 Combine all ingredients.
3 Beat for 3 minutes with an electric mixer.
4 Pour mixture on top of hot stewed apples.
5 Bake for 50–60 minutes.
6 Serve hot or cold with cream or ice cream.

Apricot shortcake

30 g/1 ounce butter
3 tablespoons castor sugar
1 egg, lightly beaten
3 tablespoons soy flour

60 g rice flour (½ cup)
⅓ cup milk
1 teaspoon baking powder
1 can apricot halves (drained)

1 Preheat oven to 175°C (350°F).
2 Grease 20 cm (8") pie plate.
3 Cream butter and sugar, gradually beat in egg.
4 Sift flours and baking powder.
5 Fold in flour and milk alternately, mix well.
6 Place half mixture in prepared pie plate.
7 Cover with apricot halves.
8 Cover with remaining mixture.
9 Bake for approximately 40–50 minutes.

Variation
Use pears, peaches or plums instead of apricots.

Baked carob pudding

1 tablespoon butter (rounded
   measure)
½ cup sugar
2 eggs separated

1 tablespoon carob powder (rounded
   measure)
1 cup milk
3 tablespoons pure maize corn flour

1 Preheat oven to 175°C (350°F).
2 Grease 20 cm (8") pie dish.
3 Cream butter and sugar.
4 Add egg yolks and beat well.
5 Add sifted flour and carob.
6 Add milk and mix thoroughly.
7 Fold in stiffly beaten egg whites.
8 Pour into pie dish and stand in tray of water.
9 Bake for approximately 1 hour until set.

Chocolate macaroon pie

Pie shell

2 egg whites
pinch of cream of tartar
½ cup sugar

½ cup coconut, desiccated
1 teaspoon vanilla

1 Preheat oven to 150°C (300°F).
2 Add egg white and cream of tartar, beat until stiff.
3 Gradually add sugar, coconut, and vanilla.
4 Spread over bottom and sides of lightly greased 20 cm (8") pie plate.
5 Bake for 35–40 minutes.
6 Cool thoroughly before filling with chocolate filling.

Filling

2 egg yolks
2 tablespoons sugar
3 tablespoons hot water
1¼ cups milk

3 level teaspoons gelatine
60 g/2 ounces grated dark chocolate
1 teaspoon lemon juice.

1 Put chocolate, milk and sugar in saucepan.
2 Stir over low heat until melted, remove from heat.
3 Beat egg yolks well, add to chocolate mixture.
4 Return to heat and stir until mixture thickens, *do not boil.*
5 Cool.
6 Dissolve gelatine in hot water.
7 Add lemon juice.
8 Blend with chocolate mixture.
9 Pour into macaroon pie shell.
10 Leave to cool.
11 Serve sprinkled with extra coconut.

Chocolate pudding

Gluten Free
(check
ingredients
of chocolate)

120 g/4 ounces milk chocolate   2 cups milk
¼ cup castor sugar   2 lightly beaten eggs
3 tablespoons pure maize corn flour   1 teaspoon vanilla

1 Mix together sugar, corn flour, milk and eggs.
2 Stir over low heat until mixture thickens.
3 Add chopped chocolate and stir until melted.
4 Simmer for 2 minutes.
5 Add vanilla.
6 Pour into individual dishes.
7 Chill several hours before serving garnished with grated chocolate
   and fresh cream.

Creamy tropical rice

Gluten Free

Serves 6–8

5 cups milk   1 teaspoon vanilla
⅔ cup rice   large can crushed pineapple (drained)
½ cup sugar (optional)   300 ml/10 ounces thickened cream

1   Put milk in large saucepan, bring just to boil.
2   Gradually add rice, stirring constantly.
3   Reduce heat, cover and simmer until milk is absorbed (50–60
    minutes), stirring frequently.
4   Remove pan from heat.
5   Add sugar and vanilla, mix well.
6   Cool.
7   Beat cream.
8   Fold drained pineapple and cream into rice.
9   Spoon into serving bowl.
10 Refrigerate until needed.

Variation
For a sugar free alternative omit sugar and use unsweetened pineapple.

73

Custard tart

½ quantity sweet barley pastry (see
   recipe page 56)
3 eggs
2 tablespoons sugar

1 cup milk
¼ teaspoon vanilla
grated nutmeg

1 Preheat oven to 200°C (400°F).
2 Line a greased 23 cm (9") tart plate with pastry.
3 Beat eggs and sugar lightly.
4 Warm milk, add eggs and sugar, add vanilla.
5 Pour into pastry case and sprinkle with nutmeg.
6 Bake at 200°C (400°F) for 10 minutes then at 175°C (350°F) for 40 minutes.

Diplomat pudding

4 cups wheatless bread, cubed
1 cup milk
60 g/2 ounces blanched whole almonds
60 g/2 ounces brazil nuts, halved
   (optional)
⅓ cup currants
⅓ cup sultanas

2 tablespoons pure maize corn flour
155 g/5 ounces butter or substitute
½ cup castor sugar
4 eggs, separated
2 teaspoons vanilla extract
2 tablespoons fine breadcrumbs
   (wheatless)

1 Place bread cubes in large mixing bowl.
2 Bring milk to boil, pour over bread and leave for 30 minutes.
3 Beat softened bread with a wooden spoon.
4 Add almonds, brazil nuts, currants, sultanas and corn flour, mix well.
5 Cream butter and sugar until light and fluffy.
6 Add egg yolks, one at a time, mixing well after each addition.
7 Mix in vanilla.
8 Add butter mixture to the bread and fruit mixture, mix well.
9 Beat egg white until firm.
10 Fold into bread mixture.
11 Grease 1½ litre (6 cup) pudding basin.
12 Sprinkle inside of basin with breadcrumbs.
13 Spoon mixture into basin, cover with well-secured, greased foil.
14 Place basin in saucepan of boiling water so that water level reaches approximately half way up the side of the basin.
15 Steam for two hours, checking water level occasionally. When water needs to be topped up, use *boiling* water only.

Fruit queen pudding

1 cup wheatless breadcrumbs
4 tablespoons jam
2 eggs
1 rounded tablespoon pure maize corn
   flour

2 cups milk
4 tablespoons castor sugar
2 cups diced fruit, fresh or canned

1 Preheat oven to 150°C (300°F).
2 Mix breadcrumbs and jam, place in ovenproof dish.
3 Separate eggs.
4 Mix corn flour with a small amount of the milk and stir until smooth.
5 Combine yolks, remaining milk, 2 tablespoons sugar and corn flour together in a saucepan.
6 Mix until smooth.
7 Heat gently until mixture thickens. Do not boil.
8 Pour over crumbs.
9 Bake for approximately 15 minutes until firm.
10 Place drained fruit over custard mixture.
11 Whip egg whites until stiff, fold in remaining sugar.
12 Pile onto fruit and custard.
13 Bake for 15 minutes at 175°C (350°F).
14 Serve hot.

Hot fruit salad crunch

Serves 4

250 g/8 ounces mixed dried fruit,
   chopped

1 cup water

1 Combine fruit salad and water in saucepan.
2 Cook until fruit is soft, approximately 20 minutes.
3 Place in pie dish.

Crunch

4 tablespoons raw sugar
2 rounded tablespoons butter
½ cup rolled oats (rye or barley
   flakes)

½ cup coconut

1 Preheat oven to 175°C (350°F).
2 Cream sugar and butter.
3 Mix oats and coconut.
4 Sprinkle on cooked fruit salad.
5 Bake until golden brown, approximately 15 minutes.
6 Serve hot or cold.

Lemon cheesecake

Base

1½ cups crushed corn flakes (measure   125 g/4 ounces butter
   after crushing)   1 tablespoon sugar
½ cup desiccated coconut   1 tablespoon milk

1 Grease a 20 cm (8") pie plate.
2 Put corn flakes and coconut in a large bowl.
3 Mix remaining ingredients in a saucepan.
4 Stir over low heat until melted and thoroughly mixed.
5 Pour over dry ingredients, mix well.
6 Press into prepared plate.
7 Store in refrigerator while making the filling.

Filling

1 packet lemon gelatine dessert   250 g/8 ounces cream cheese
2 tablespoons boiling water   400 g/14 ounce can sweetened
½ cup lemon juice   condensed milk, chilled
1 teaspoon grated lemon rind   1 teaspoon vanilla

1 Dissolve jelly in boiling water.
2 Add lemon juice and cool.
3 Whip cheese until soft and creamy.
4 Add condensed milk and mix for one minute.
5 Add vanilla and cooled jelly.
6 Pour over prepared base.
7 Refrigerate until set.

Variation

For a sugar free, low fat alternative:

Base

Leave out sugar, use sugarless corn flakes from health food store and increase milk to 1½ tablespoons, or use base of Passionfruit yoghurt slice (see recipe page 41), but *please note this base is not gluten free.*

Filling

Replace first three ingredients with 250 g/8 ounces smooth ricotta cheese, 1 packet artificially sweetened lemon jelly, or 1 tablespoon gelatine, and 1 cup skim milk yoghurt.

Lemon meringue pie

½ quantity sweet barley pastry (see recipe page 56)
2 level tablespoons pure maize corn flour
2 lemons

6 tablespoons water
6 tablespoons castor sugar
2 eggs
1 tablespoon castor sugar, extra for meringue top

1 Line 20 cm (8") pie dish with pastry.
2 Mix together corn flour, lemon juice, grated rind of one lemon and water in saucepan.
3 Bring to boil and simmer for 1 minute.
4 Add sugar and stir until sugar has dissolved.
5 When cool add yolks of eggs.
6 Reheat and pour over pastry base.
7 Preheat oven to 120°C (250°F).
8 Whip egg whites stiffly.
9 Fold in the extra castor sugar.
10 Pile on top of pie.
11 Bake for approximately 15 minutes or until meringue is pale brown in colour and crisp.
12 Serve hot or cold.

Lemon tapioca

Gluten Free

1 cup tapioca
3 cups water
2 lemons

3 tablespoons golden syrup
3 tablespoons brown sugar

1 Combine tapioca and water in saucepan.
2 Boil until clear.
3 Add juice and grated rind of lemons, golden syrup and sugar.
4 Simmer, stirring occasionally until mixture is quite thick.
5 Remove from heat and allow to cool.
6 Pour into wet dish and chill.
7 Serve with or without cream.

Orange or lemon delicious pudding

1 tablespoon butter
4 tablespoons sugar
2 eggs

2 tablespoons pure maize corn flour
2 lemons or 2 oranges
1 ¼ cups milk

1 Preheat oven to 175°C (350°F).
2 Cream butter and sugar.
3 Add egg yolks, sifted flour, grated rind and juice of fruit, mix well.
4 Gradually add milk and stir thoroughly.
5 Beat egg whites stiffly.
6 Fold into pudding.
7 Pour into buttered ovenproof dish.
8 Bake, standing in a dish of water for 30 minutes.

Plum pudding

¼ cup mixed candied dried fruits
½ cup raisins
½ cup sultanas
½ cup currants
¼ cup dates (pitted and chopped)
¾ cup orange juice or water

2 eggs
1 ripe mashed banana
¾ cup brown rice flour
½ cup rye flour
2 teaspoons baking powder
¼ teaspoon nutmeg
½ teaspoon cinnamon

1 Grease a 1 litre (4 cup) basin.
2 Place fruit and water or juice in saucepan, bring to the boil and simmer for 2 minutes, then cool.
3 Add eggs and banana to fruit mixture.
4 Add flours, baking powder and spices and mix well.
5 Pour into basin and cover with well-secured, greased foil.
6 Place in a saucepan of boiling water so that water level reaches approximately halfway up the side of the basin.
7 Steam for 1¼ hours. Do not let saucepan boil dry. When adding more water make sure it is boiling.

Variation
For a gluten free alternative substitute soy flour for the rye flour. Reduce cooking time to 1 hour.

Tapioca plum pudding

½ cup tapioca
1 cup milk
1 cup soft, wheatless breadcrumbs
½ cup raisins

½ cup sultanas
½ cup sugar
¼ teaspoon bicarbonate of soda
2 tablespoons melted butter

1 Place sago and milk in large bowl to soak overnight.
2 Mix in remaining ingredients.
3 Pour mixture into greased 1 litre (4 cup) basin, cover with well-secured, greased foil.
4 Place basin in saucepan of *boiling* water so that water level reaches approximately half way up the side of the basin.
5 Steam for 2 to 2½ hours, checking water level occasionally. When water needs to be topped up, use *boiling* water only.

Gluten Free

Simple meringue case

Approximately 20 cm (8") diameter

3 egg whites
pinch salt
¾ cup castor sugar

¼ cup granulated sugar (white
    sugar)
1 tablespoon pure maize corn flour
1 teaspoon lemon juice

1 Preheat oven to 150°C (300°F).
2 Beat egg whites and salt until stiff and dry.
3 Add castor sugar gradually, beating well between each addition
   (make sure sugar is completely dissolved).
4 Mix together white sugar and corn flour.
5 Lightly fold into meringue mixture with lemon juice.
6 Spread thinly (1 cm/½") over very lightly greased pavlova (or
   pizza) tray.
7 Spoon swirls around the edge.
8 Bake for approximately 30–40 minutes.
9 Decorate with whipped cream and fresh fruit.

Suggested toppings
Use strawberries; kiwi fruit.

Breakfast

Granola

Serves 4

1 cup rolled oats
½ cup rolled rye (rye flakes)
½ cup rolled barley (barley flakes)
¼ cup buckwheat kernels
½ cup chopped nuts

¼ cup sesame seeds
½ cup chopped dried fruit (apples,
   apricots, sultanas, etc.)
2 tablespoons oil (or melted butter).

1 Oil a flat baking tray.
2 Mix all dry ingredients except fruit and place in tray.
3 Sprinkle with oil.
4 Bake at 160°C (325°F) for approximately 30 minutes, stirring frequently, until golden in colour.
5 Cool and add dried fruit.
6 Store in airtight container.
7 Serve with milk.

Some serving suggestions
Top with sliced banana, or grated raw apple, or coconut, or raw sugar,
or any combination of these.

Porridge

Serves 4

2 cups rolled oats	*½ cup sultanas (optional)*
5 cups boiling water	*salt to taste*

1 Mix ingredients and allow to stand for 10 minutes if possible. (To save time in the morning, you could soak ingredients overnight. The porridge will also be creamier.)
2 Boil for 10–15 minutes.
3 Serve with milk and raw sugar.

Variations
Use hulled millet (soak overnight) for a gluten free alternative; millet meal also for a gluten free alternative; ½ rolled oats and ½ rye flakes; ½ oatmeal and ½ millet meal; ½ millet meal and ½ buckwheat meal; or any combination of the above.
Note: You will not need as much 'meal' as rolled grains, soaking is not necessary with the 'meals', and cooking time should be reduced to 5–7 minutes. So, for 'meals' follow the steps listed below:
1 Put ½ cup meal (any combinations) in saucepan.
2 Stir in 1½ cups water gradually.
3 Stir constantly over low heat until mixture thickens.
4 Simmer for 5–7 minutes.

Variation
For a sugar free alternative serve with stewed fruit instead of sugar.

Muesli porridge

Serves 2

4 tablespoons oatmeal	*1 tablespoon raisins or sultanas*
2 tablespoons buckwheat kernels	*2 tablespoons mixed, dried, chopped*
2 tablespoons unhulled millet	* fruit*
2 tablespoons skim milk powder (or	*1 cup water*
* powdered soy milk)*	*desiccated coconut (optional)*
1 tablespoon chopped nuts	*raw sugar (optional)*

1 Mix all ingredients except coconut and sugar in saucepan.
2 Heat gently until thick and creamy.
3 Sprinkle with coconut and raw sugar (optional).
4 Serve with milk.

Variations
For a gluten free variation substitute millet meal for the oatmeal. Check for buckwheat tolerance. For a sugar free alternative omit sugar.

Roasted muesli

Serves 4

2 cups rolled oats	*3 tablespoons oil*
½ cup coconut	*2 tablespoons honey*
½ cup sunflower seeds	*1–1½ cups mixed sultanas, raisins,*
½ cup sesame seeds	*currants, chopped*
¼ cup chopped nuts	

1 Place all dry ingredients except fruit in a baking tray.
2 Mix thoroughly and sprinkle with oil and honey.
3 Bake at 175°C (350°F) stirring frequently.
4 Cool, add fruit.
5 Store in airtight container.
6 Serve with milk or juice.

Variation
Add ¼ cup each of buckwheat kernels, and unhulled millet.
For a gluten free alternative use soy flakes in place of rolled oats.
For a sugar free alternative omit honey.

Unroasted muesli

1 Refer to ingredients for roasted muesli (see above) but leave out oil
   and honey.
2 Mix remaining ingredients thoroughly.
3 Store in an airtight container.
4 Serve with milk or juice.
5 Top with honey or raw sugar; grated apple or sliced banana; or
   fresh or canned peaches, pears or apricots.

Sugar Free
Swiss breakfast

Serves 1

½ cup oatmeal	*½ banana*
½ cup orange juice	*½ apple*
1 tablespoon sultanas	*½ tablespoon chopped nuts*

1 Soak oatmeal in orange juice overnight.
2 Slice banana and grate apple.
3 Add apple, banana, sultanas and nuts to oatmeal mixture.
4 Serve either plain or with cream or yoghurt.

Index, all recipes

Index, gluten-free recipes

Index, sugar-free recipes